m

The Kremlin and Labor:

A Study in National Security Policy

CE

The Kremlin and Labor:

A Study in National Security Policy

PUBLISHED BY
**Crane, Russak &
Company, Inc.**
NEW YORK

Roy Godson

National Strategy
Information Center, Inc.

The Kremlin and Labor

Published in the United States by
Crane, Russak & Company, Inc.
347 Madison Avenue
New York, N.Y. 10017

Copyright © 1977 by
National Strategy Information Center,
Inc.
111 East 58th Street
New York, N.Y. 10022

Library Edition: ISBN 0-8448-1274-9
Paperbound Edition: ISBN
0-8448-1225-0
LC 77-85317

Strategy Paper No. 32

Printed in the United States of America

Table of Contents

Preface

While Western analysts devote a great deal of effort to the study of Soviet objectives and policy instruments, almost no attention has been paid to the role of labor in Soviet national security policy. But as Dr. Roy Godson demonstrates in this NSIC Strategy Paper, labor is indeed a significant instrument of Soviet policy and worthy of much more intensive study. Not only does the Kremlin claim that the labor movement is an important means for helping to shift the world balance of power (or "the correlation of forces") in its favor. Moscow also devotes considerable human and material resources to influence this strategic sector throughout the non-Communist world. Moreover, these efforts have been stepped up in recent years, and still appear to be expanding, especially in Asia, Africa, and Latin America.

Whether the Kremlin will be able to capitalize fully on its investments in this sector will depend, in part, on the reactions of Western governmental and nongovernmental organizations. But it is only on the basis of a much greater understanding of the subject that the West can develop an effective strategy for dealing with Soviet efforts to use labor as an instrument of policy. Dr. Godson's study is an important initial contribution to this end.

Dr. Godson was educated at Middlebury College, the London School of Economics, and Columbia University. He is currently Associate Professor of Government and Director of the International Labor Program at Georgetown University, and a Research Associate of the National Strategy Information Center specializing in transnational relations and national security affairs. His book *American Labor and European Politics* was published last year.

Frank R. Barnett, *President*
National Strategy Information Center, Inc.

November 1977

Summary

Although some people argue that the Kremlin has lost interest in the use of organized labor as an instrument of policy, this does not appear to be the case. While the Soviet Union has acquired super-power status and may now place greater emphasis on traditional instruments of statecraft, Moscow continues to employ a transnational strategy as well—attempting to alter the balance of power by influencing important nongovernmental sectors throughout the world. For the Kremlin, the labor movement is one means of affecting political conditions in the non-Communist world. Soviet leaders and analysts stress the importance of the subject; and past Soviet practice indicates that labor has been seen and used as a political tool. Today, the Kremlin continues to devote considerable attention, resources, and manpower to utilizing labor to affect the global power struggle.

Soviet efforts, however, have not always produced significant results. In the developed countries, they have had only mixed success at best. On the whole, they have not been able to secure major influence in the unions of Northern Europe, although they have been able to use labor on occasion to promote the Soviet concept of detente, to weaken the region economically, and to lower European interest in defense expenditures. In Southern Europe, however, they have supported—and on the whole have been the benficiaries of—Communist control of major sections of the labor movement.

In the less developed areas, Moscow and the local Communist Parties have not been able to gain control of organized labor—with certain notable exceptions. But as the years pass, the Kremlin is training and financing many thousands of union officials; and in some strategic areas such as Southern Africa and the Persian Gulf, there is little in the way of a countervailing Western presence.

We need to know much more about the circumstances under which Moscow's efforts are and are not effective, and why the subject has attracted so little attention in the West. Only then can we decide what precisely to do about the Soviet effort to use labor as one means of shifting the global balance.

The Kremlin and Labor:

A Study in National Security Policy

Introduction

Few Western specialist have paid attention to the role of organized labor as an instrument of Soviet national security policy. While many agree that the Soviet leadership employs political tools in addition to military, economic, and cultural instruments, the role of organized labor has been ignored completely or mentioned only briefly in discussions of Soviet objectives and methods, or in assessing Soviet influence in the non-Communist world.[1]

The primary purpose of this study is to demonstrate that organized labor is indeed a significant instrument of Soviet policy. While the importance of the subject and the objectives and tactics employed have varied over time, the behavior of the current Soviet leadership particularly reveals their belief that labor can be a useful means for helping to shift the power balance in their favor. Moscow is presently investing considerable human and material resources to influence the labor sector throughout the non-Communist world, and some of these efforts already have begun to pay handsome dividends.

The second purpose of the study is to draw policy implications from these conclusions. One which stands out clearly is that the Soviet

---

[1] A cursory examination of the index of any recent study of Soviet policy leads to this conclusion. See, for example, Richard Pipes, *Soviet Strategy in Europe* (New York: Crane, Russak, 1976), and Alvin Z. Rubinstein, *Soviet and Chinese Influence in the Third World* (New York: Praeger, 1975). Even US government publications usually do not even mention labor; see, for example, the unclassified annual series on *Communist Aid to the Less Developed Countries.*

use of organized labor, and the Western reaction to it, merit much closer study and attention. If we are to understand fully the importance of the subject and draw correct policy conclusions, we need to know much more about the role of labor in domestic and international affairs, how the Soviets are operating, and how effective they can be. It would also be helpful to understand Western governmental and nongovernmental reaction to Soviet activities in the labor field. Outside of the AFL-CIO, however, the subject is now more or less ignored in the United States. Why? Do business and government circles believe Soviet efforts to gain control of the labor movement to be of little importance? Or, as some have suggested, do they see it as a useful means of preventing the rise of what otherwise might be a powerful international social force opposed to "detente"?

A comprehensive understanding of Soviet labor activities would also provide us with another indicator of the direction of overall Soviet behavior. It can be used to inform us about Soviet objectives and methods on a global level as well as in a given region. As is discussed below, for example, Moscow is making considerable efforts overtly and covertly to bolster and increase the strength of unions controlled by the European Communist Parties. This leads to the conclusion that far from being completely unhappy with "Eurocommunism," it is still trying to increase the strength of what it clearly regards as an important pro-Soviet force in Europe. Thus the study of Soviet labor activities is not only important for those concerned with nonmilitary instruments; it also has a more general application for students of overall Soviet national security policy.[2]

---

[2] The international role of Soviet labor organizations may also tell us something about internal struggles in the Kremlin. In the 1920s, for example, Mikhail Tomsky, a member of the Politburo and Chairman of the All-Union Central Council of Trade Unions (AUCCTU), apparently attempted to use the AUCCTU's international contacts to increase the labor organization's independence from the Communist Party and enhance his ability to support the anti-Trotsky line in the Politburo. See Daniel F. Calhoun, *The United Front, The TUC and the Russians, 1923–28* (London: Cambridge University Press, 1976), especially pp. 22–23. Some 50 years later, another Chairman of the AUCCTU, also a member of the Politburo, Alexandr Shelepin, may have attempted to use international labor diplomacy to bolster his position and move the Soviet elite in his preferred direction. On possible differences between Shelepin and some of his Politburo colleagues, see, for example, Ilana Dimant, *Pravda and Trud, Divergent Attitudes Towards the Middle East,* Research Paper No. 3, Soviet and East European Research Center, Hebrew University, 1972.

A second major implication is that there is a need for action. What those concerned with preventing the Soviets from increasing their influence in the non-Communist world should do is beyond the purview of this study. But, as the data presented here suggest, the Soviets are seeking to use labor to reduce US and Western power and influence throughout the world. Sometimes they have deliberately sought short-term gains. But generally they see the labor sector in long-range terms, too; and they may gain much more over the long run than they have during the past few years. In some regions, besides launching humanitarian programs to help foreign workers, American nongovernmental organizations such as the AFL-CIO are doing a great deal to stem the spread of Soviet or Soviet-backed influence. But in other areas, there is no American or Western presence to counteract or contain Soviet activitives, and the consequences of this situation are unlikely to benefit the West.

The present study is divided into two parts. The first is concerned with current Soviet perspectives on the role of labor in international affairs. How do the Soviets think about the use of organized labor? Soviet views on some aspects of this subject have shifted from time to time, usually as a reflection of changing foreign policy perspectives. But by and large, they have been fairly consistent in the 1970s.

For the most part, information about these perspectives can be found in current Soviet sources. The writings of Soviet leaders and senior Party and labor analysts generally provide a good indicator of Soviet perspectives. On the other hand, Soviet views on the specific means by which labor in foreign countries can be used as an instrument of national security policy are not discussed publicly. Here it is necessary to study past Soviet practice. For decades, the Soviet leadership has used organized labor to influence political and military conditions abroad—and almost never discussed the subject publicly. To some extent, specific usages must have become institutionalized in Soviet thinking. Unless they believe that their past behavior was drastically mistaken, and except where they have departed considerably from previous practice, their past behavior may be used as a reasonable guide to current perspectives.

Some will assert that Soviet statements are mere rhetoric, and cannot be taken seriously. This may be true, of course, and few students of national security policy would take the statements of any actor as the sole indicator of policy. But such official statements do offer one indication that the leadership believes organized labor to be of considerable significance in world affairs. Another indication can be found in Soviet practice. After discussing policymaking and implementation in the labor area, and the role of the Soviet-controlled World Federation of Trade Unions (WFTU), Moscow's efforts to use organized labor to help tip the world balance of power in its favor will be described and assessed. The data are drawn from a wide variety of Soviet and Western sources, including interviews conducted in 1975, 1976, and 1977 with current and former Soviet and WFTU officials and Western and non-Western union leaders.

It should be noted that in this study the term "Soviet," as opposed to "Russian," refers to the USSR, its policies, and its officials. The term "labor organizations" refers to workers' organizations controlled by ruling Communist Parties or other governmental elites. An effort will be made throughout to distinguish "labor organizations" from what in the West are referred to as "trade unions"—organizations designed to protect workers' interests which are not controlled by a governmental elite.[3]

Finally, the author wishes to acknowledge the assistance of numerous scholars and practitioners of international affairs, as well as scores of trade union officials, in the preparation of this study. He is also indebted to the research assistance of Melanie Stern and David Dorn, and the skill, patience, and encouragement of other members of the staff of Georgetown University's International Labor Program.

---

[3] On the complexities of the distinction between trade unions and labor organizations, see William A. Douglas, *Trade Union Freedom and Human Rights, An Index Approach to Measurement,* Institute for Conflict and Policy Studies, Special Report Series, October 1977.

1

Soviet Perspectives on the Role of Labor in World Politics

The Significance of Labor

For the Soviet leadership, the "working class" and its institutions are the most important forces in history. They maintain that working class parties, labor organizations, and trade unions are crucially important in world politics. As these institutions are "strengthened" and "unified" under the leadership of Communist Parties throughout the world, ultimately the balance—or what the Soviets call the "correlation"—of forces will tip decisively in favor of socialism and lead to the demise of the capitalist powers.

In the Soviet Union, the Communist Party of the Soviet Union (CPSU) is the most important working class institution. Because the working class is in power, the CPSU "represents" the interests of all the people in both domestic and foreign affairs. All other institutions must follow its "leadership." This is especially important for major social organizations such as the national "trade union" center, the All-Union Central Council of Trade Unions (AUCCTU).[4]

In fact, the labor organizations insist that they follow unswervingly the precise foreign policy directives of the Party. At the 16th Congress

---

[4] See, for example, T.S. Yampolskaya, *Social Organizations in the Soviet Union* (Moscow: Progress Publishers, 1975), p. 53. "The unions perform their tasks under the direct leadership of the CPSU and in close contact with the system of Soviets and the sectoral apparatus of the state administration."

of the AUCCTU, for example, the "delegates declared their total support for the CPSU Central Committee's political course and activity, and assured it that trade union organizations would make every effort to implement the decisions of the 25th CPSU Congress."[5] Another example of this unswerving support can be found in periodic AUCCTU Plenum statements. "The AUCCTU Plenum assured the CPSU Central Committee that the Soviet trade unions will continue to make every effort to contribute, through their international activity, to the successful, practical implementation of the CPSU's foreign policy."[6] "The Plenum unanimously approved the draft of the CPSU Central Committee for the 25th CPSU Central Committee Plenum and the conclusions and propositions contained in Brezhnev's speech."[7]

Outside the Soviet Union and other states ruled by Communist parties (the "world Socialist system"), the Soviet leadership sees the AUCCTU's main task—in addition to promoting Soviet foreign policy in general—as advancing and strengthening working class unity. This means, of course, unifying the working class under the leadership of its most "advanced elements," the Communist Parties, as well as undermining non-Communist leaders who are alleged to be splitting the working class. The stress on working class unity under the leadership of the Communist Party is one of the most important points in Soviet doctrine. For example, an authoritative book edited by V. V. Zagladin, the first deputy head of the CPSU International Department, maintains that:[8]

> The struggle for working class unity is one of the major tasks confronting the world Communist movement. In many respects, the prospects for peace, democracy, and socialism hinge on the accomplishment of that task. The unification of all workers in a single class force is a most important principle in the strategy and tactics of the world's Communists.

Important promulgators of Soviet doctrine in this area such as Zagladin (who was promoted in 1976 to be a candidate member of the

---

[5] *Trud,* March 23, 1977.
[6] "An AUCCTU Plenum," *ibid.,* May 23, 1975.
[7] Moscow Radio's Domestic Service, Foreign Broadcast Information Service (hereafter referred to as FBIS), December 30, 1975.
[8] V. V. Zagladin, ed., *The World Communist Movement* (Moscow: Progress Publishers, 1973), p. 188.

Central Committee), and other specialists on the international labor movement, frequently are fond of citing Lenin to make the same point:[9]

> Unity is infinitely precious, and infinitely important to the working class. Disunited the workers are nothing. United they are everything.

They also cite statements such at that of the 1969 meeting of Communist and Workers Parties to demonstrate that the International Communist movement recognizes this:[10]

> The restoration of unity in the trade union movement, where it is split, as well as on the international scale, is essential for heightening the role of the working class in political life and the successful defense of its interests.

But to achieve unity, the Soviet leaders think they have to eradicate the divisions in the working class which lead some workers to follow Communists, others to follow the Social Democrats and the "petty bourgeois and bourgeois parties," and still others to stand outside the political struggle altogether. Why this disunity? For the Soviets, one must first consider the nature of the working class. It is derived from the heterogeneous racial, ethnic, religious, and economic composition of the work force. Secondly, as they see it, there are the activities of the "bourgeoisie," which, fearing the power of the united working class, does everything in its power to "bribe" the workers and prevent the development of working class unity.

The struggle for unity among working class political parties, particularly Socialist and Communist parties, is one of the highest priorities. But unity in the labor movement is also of major significance. This significance, Moscow maintains, results from trade unions being the largest mass nonparty organization, with a membership embracing workers of the most varying views.[11] Their importance has increased along with their growing membership. Moscow maintains that 250 million people are now members of trade unions, as opposed to 65

---

[9] Lenin, *Collected Works,* vol. 19, p. 519.
[10] Zagladin, *op. cit.,* p. 229.
[11] *Ibid.,* p. 220.

million in 1945 and 15 million in 1913. The effectiveness of the unions in the "anti-imperialist" struggle will increase, they believe, as more and more workers join unions and unity among workers with varying viewpoints is achieved. To become more effective, the trade unions— like other working class institutions—must increase their strength, overcome their own disunity, and the "splitting activities of the bourgeoisie."[12]

There are three major interrelated methods or principles through which working class institutions can be strengthened and unified both on the national and international levels. First, the workers must become deeply embroiled in the "revolutionary struggle." Unity cannot be imposed from the outside. By struggling together against the prevailing economic order and defending their interests, the workers will gradually understand the need for unification. To emphasize this point, Lenin is often quoted: "Unity must be won, and only the workers, the class-conscious workers themselves, can win it—by stubborn and persistent effort.[13]

Second, and related to the revolutionary struggle, there must be close cooperation between the unions and the workers' "most advanced representatives," the Communist Party. As Zagladin puts it: "Wherever Communist influence on the trade unions is stronger, the proletariat's class consciousness is greater, as is its militancy, and trade union participation in the political struggle is broader."[14] Cooperation with Communists prevents the trade unions from becoming "class collaborators" (who merely try to improve the lives of the workers in small ways), and reduces the effectiveness of the splitting tactics of the bourgeoisie.

Just what kind of relations Communists are to maintain with the unions, however, is not clearly stated in Soviet sources. On one hand, the unions are to remain "independent." They are not to become "branches of the Party" lest this lead to the "isolation of the trade unions" and their "divorce from the masses." Experience has shown, Zagladin observes, that this will happen with the organization of "purely Communist trade unions." On the other hand, the extent to

---

[12] Georgii Kanaev, *Soviet Trade Unions and the International Trade Union Movement* (Moscow: Novosti Press, 1970), pp. 6–7. Kanaev was deputy head of the AUCCTU's International Affairs Department.
[13] *Ibid.,* p. 3.
[14] Zagladin, *op. cit.,* p. 220.

which Communists are to control the unions is vague. Communists "are working for the closest possible contacts with the trade unions and are firmly opposed to any underestimation of Communist activities in trade union ranks. Communists working in the trade unions are out to have the latter best accomplish the tasks confronting them."[15] Zagladin and others then go on to cite Lenin on these tasks.

Lenin, of course, argued against trade union "neutrality," that is, restricting the trade unions to economic concerns and having them remain neutral on political matters. Instead, the unions were to involve themselves in direct political activities. They were to serve as political schools for the working class and as a means for defending their political as well as economic interests. In these tasks, Communists were to work closely with the unions and link them with the Party's "aims and ideals."[16]

The third principle to be used in strengthening and unifying the workers is "proletarian internationalism." Proletarian internationalism, a leading Soviet labor official has stated, "is a major ideological basis of the entire activity of Soviet trade unions."[17] This means apparently that working people throughout the world have common interests and help each other in the attainment of their common objectives. Soviet workers and their organizations recognize these interests and are struggling to assist workers and their organizations throughout the world. As a result, proletarian internationalism has become "a powerful instrument in uniting the working class, all working people and revolutionary and democratic forces in various countries, in their struggle against the exploiting classes."[18]

A variety of specific tactics can be subsumed under the rubric of proletarian internationalism. Among the most significant are (a) defending the Soviet revolution and its significance as a worldwide social force; (b) material and fraternal assistance to working class forces throughout the world; and (c) dialogue on both the national

---

[15] *Ibid.*

[16] For Lenin's views about trade unions and politics, see *V. I. Lenin on Trade Unions, A Collection of Articles and Speeches* (Moscow: Progress Publishers, 1970); and Thomas Hammond, *Lenin on Trade Unions and Revolution* (New York: Columbia University Press, 1957).

[17] K. A. Guseinov, *Trade Union Association: USSR, Asia and Africa* (Moscow: Nauka Publishers, 1967), p. 5.

[18] Zagladin, *op. cit.,* p. 441.

and international levels with trade unions representing different points of view on the need for cooperation and unity.

With this general perspective in mind, the Soviet leadership maintains that, in general (that is, with some exceptions), the working class in capitalist countries is the most promising revolutionary force today, and strengthening and unifying this element is very important. Soviet analysts state that this class comprises about 230 million people, and for the most part is located in North America, Western Europe, and Japan. It is, they insist, the most organized class and has acquired rich experience of the class struggle. The objective preconditions are ripe for a transition from capitalism to socialism in these countries; but the revolutionary process is developing slowly and unevenly, "since the revolutionary movement is confronted by a highly organized and experienced enemy."[19] One of the major long-term tasks of trade unions in these countries is to "curb the power of the monopolies." The unions are to do this by increasing their influence over all phases of economic and political life, especially by demands for nationalization and control of key industries. If the unions and other working class institutions acquire control of the economy, they will be in a strong position to unify the workers.

From the late 1920s up until approximately the death of Stalin, the Kremlin—in its doctrine, at least—made little distinction between the Third World and the capitalist countries. With the 20th Party Congress in 1956, Moscow acknowledged that all states were not necessarily members of either the Socialist or the capitalist camp. There were "in-between" states in the Third World, and they presented the Soviet Union with new and different problems, as well as important opportunities. Specifically, their nationalism and reaction to Western colonial rule made them natural allies for the major anti-imperialist powers—the Soviet Union and its allies. Indeed, in Soviet judgment the "national liberation forces" in the Third World became not only "one of the main elements of the world anti-imperialist movement," but allies of the Communist states in a joint offensive against imperialism and capitalism as a system of social relations.[20]

---

[19] *Ibid.,* p. 94.
[20] Leon Gouré and Morris Rothenberg, *Soviet Penetration of Latin America* (Miami: Center for Advanced International Studies, 1975), p. 10. The entire first chapter of this monograph is devoted to changing Soviet perspectives on the Third World and particularly Latin America.

For the non-Western people, this involved, in the first stage, freeing themselves from colonial rule, and in the second stage, after formal independence was obtained, establishing their genuine independence from neocolonialism and the national bourgeoisie. The second stage of the national liberation struggle and the governments it has produced has received various Soviet designations—national democracy, revolutionary democracy, people's democracy, noncapitalist path, Socialist orientation—to define stages somewhere between capitalism and a Socialist state.

Nevertheless, Moscow insists that until a Communist Party has obtained a monopoly of power or a "revolutionary party" becomes Marxist-Leninist in theory and in practice, all these regimes must be considered as creating favorable conditions for the advent of socialism. They are not in themselves Socialist. The Soviet leaders still insist that the working class and its vanguard must be in power if there is to be a completely satisfactory change. Indeed, they frequently classify a regime primarily according to the role of the Communist Party and other working class institutions. Moscow recognizes a variety of possibilities. They can range from Communist participation in government with other "democratic forces"—including those of a bourgeois character to which they have, for the moment, to concede leadership—to ideological purity in opposition. The key tactic is increasing the strength and unity of working class forces under the leadership of vanguard forces.

Current Opportunities

As the Soviets see it now, there is a distinction between most of Africa, the Middle East, and Asia, on the one hand, and Latin America on the other. These areas have a number of distinct historic, economic, and political characteristics, and as a result present different opportunities for the Soviets.

For Moscow, Africa and Asia, which only recently threw off the colonial yoke, now have an opportunity to develop along a "noncapitalist" path. They are not bound to develop along the lines of the capitalist states, nor even along lines of Latin America, which the Soviets see as basically capitalist. Instead, they can reduce the power of "international monopolies" and the private sector, and increase the influence of the Socialist camp and the state sector until they are ready for the transition to communism.

The Afro-Asian states, the Soviets maintain, still are suffering from the legacy of colonialism. During the many centuries of European rule, exploitation of the population was based on a divide-and-rule principle. Deliberately and systematically, the "colonialists fostered strife amongst the enslaved nations and tribes, and then acted as pacifiers saving them from mutual destruction."[21] The economies of these areas were converted into colonial appendages, supplying the West with raw materials. The result was economic stagnation, little industry, and a very small, weak, and poorly organized proletariat.

These circumstances led the incipient trade union movement to develop in specific directions. First, the Asian and African unions. Soviet analysts maintain, were neutral in political terms. They engaged in economic, as opposed to political, activities because their roots were in reformist Western unions. Second, they were "isolated" on the national as well as the continental scale. The same "monopoly capital" prevented them from unifying in the past, and still prevents the unification of these forces today. "Progressive forces" within various labor movements are victimized and purged, and attempts are made to prevent union leaders from learning about the Soviet model and bringing about the unification of workers on a continental basis.

In the 1970s, according to the Soviets, the main struggle of these countries is along the "noncapitalist path" of development. They have to build an anti-imperialist national democratic front of progressive forces. The precise composition and forces of the front may be different in different countries and stages, but the working class, although small now, will be the most revolutionary group in the long run. In the first stage of the liberation struggle, the overthrow of colonialism, the workers' class interests coincided in the main with the interests and struggle of the entire nation. Since then, the national bourgeoisie has begun to defend its interests to the detriment of the rest of the country. Hence, the working class now has to struggle against the remnants of imperialism from abroad and the local bourgeoisie at home. The trade unions have to be strengthened and unified on both the national and international planes as part of this effort.

For the Soviets, Latin America has special characteristics. First, it is a more advanced region. As a result of having achieved independence in the 19th century, Latin American countries embarked on

---

[21] Guseinov, *op. cit.,* p. 8.

the capitalist road to development many years ago. But this type of capitalist system was retarded by its dependence on the large industrial countries, particularly the United States, which provided it with technology and investments, and in turn became the principal markets of the region.

Soviet analysts also maintain that there is great unevenness in the economic and political development of the region. They point to different political conditions and alignments in various countries, giving rise to different revolutionary opportunities. Politically and ideologically, the Latin American regimes range through the entire spectrum of Soviet typology—from reactionary proimperialist governments (for example, Paraguay and Brazil) through nationalist-reformist bourgeois regimes (Colombia and Venezuela) to "progressive," "democratic," or even "revolutionary democratic" systems, as in Chile under Allende or represented in varying degrees by the military governments of Peru, Panama, and Ecuador.

The "contradictions" or results of these special types of societies are also somewhat different from those at work in Africa and Asia. First, there is a powerful nationalist mass movement in the continent which assumes a more or less pronounced anti-imperialist, anticapitalist character; and this does not exist in other Third World areas. The movement consists of the merged results of the contradictions between (a) the peasants and semifeudal landlords, (b) the urban proletariat and a rather highly developed bourgeoisie, and (c) the national aspirations of the people and the interests of the foreign exploiters. Second, according to Boris Ponomarev, the CPSU Secretary with responsibility for the nonruling international Communist movement, a strong working class has developed in Latin America "with considerable experience in revolutionary struggle." "All Latin American countries have Communist Parties, and in many countries they are big and influential." The social democratic movement, however, "does not have profound roots in the labor movement on the continent and does not enjoy a major influence."[22]

Moscow recognizes that the relative weakness of the Latin American Communist Parties makes it unlikely that they can attain power by themselves or through violent revolution. Instead, they are encour-

---

[22] "Topical Problems in the Theory of the World Revolutionary Process," *Kommunist* (Moscow), October 1971.

aged to seek new alliances with other "revolutionary anti-imperialist and democratic forces." "These involve the working class, peasantry, the petty and middle bourgeoisie, the patriotic military, and even such sections of the bourgeoisie which, under certain conditions, find themselves involved in contradition with monopoly capitalism and are objectively interested in opposing imperialist penetration."[23] On the other hand, "the proletariat is the most powerful social class in Latin America. . . . In a number of countries, the industrial core of the working class at enterprises employing 50 or more workers accounts for the majority of industrial workers. The Communist Parties have an overall membership of over 350,000."[24] To win leadership of the broad anti-imperialist front, the working class must overcome the disunity in its own ranks. As in other capitalist areas, this is caused by what the Soviets call the "splitting activities" of the bourgeoisie, overt and covert anticommunism and anti-Sovietism, and the import of petty bourgeois ideology, which reduces the class consciousness of the workers and makes them interested in reformist programs and institutions.

Apart from working class forces in separate regions, the Soviets also believe that the international labor movement on its own can play a role in shifting the balance of forces further in their favor. They believe that unity among the global internationals (the World Federation of Trade Unions, the International Confederation of Free Trade Unions, and the World Confederation of Labor), regional labor organizations (the International Confederation of Arab Trade Unions, the Organization of African Trade Union Unity, the European Trade Union Confederation, and the Latin American regional labor bodies), as well as industrial internationals (see the Appendix) can play a role in weakening the West and furthering "world revolution." As a Soviet international labor specialist put it: "Soviet trade unions believe that unity of trade union action on a national, regional, and international scale will help to undermine the political and economic power of the monopolies. . . . Soviet trade unions believe that the tendency toward unity of different units (holding different political views) of the international trade union movement is an objective

---

[23] Zagladin, *op. cit.*, p. 340.
[24] *Ibid.*, p. 346.

factor directly connected with the class interests of the working people and their vital needs. This tendency, despite all the machinations of the splitters of the proletariat, has always been the basis of the international trade union movement."[25]

Soviet leaders see unprecedented opportunities to achieve their objectives in the present world situation. They maintain that the Socialist world is gaining strength, while the capitalist world becomes increasingly unable to solve its problems; and thus the working people in both capitalist and Third World areas will come to realize the need for unity and a transition to socialism. As Ponomarev put it, the two most important processes during the 1970s have been "the growing might of countries of the Socialist community, their vigorous action together with all the peace forces against imperialist aggression, for detente and international security; and second, the mounting struggle of the working class and working people generally in the capitalist countries, of the ex-colonial peoples and anti-imperialist movement as a whole. Developing in interconnection, these two cardinal social processes have substantially changed the international situation in favor of peace and socialism."[26]

The Soviets maintain that in addition to their increased military strength, they and the East European states have entered a new and higher phase of economic and political development. They also maintain that the achievements of "existing socialism made possible the historical change from the Cold War to detente and the consolidation of the principles of the peaceful coexistence of states with differing social systems."[27]

But "peaceful coexistence" for the Kremlin remains, as it has more or less since the time of Lenin, a strategy or stage that can be used to bring about the destruction of capitalism. As both Lenin and Stalin pointed out, states with different social systems can coexist for limited periods of time, and peaceful coexistence should be used to strengthen the Communist camp. The major difference in peaceful coexistence now as compared with earlier periods, Soviet writers maintain, is that

---

[25] Kanaev, *op. cit.,* pp. 55–56.
[26] Boris Ponomarev, "The World Situation and the Revolutionary Process," *World Marxist Review,* June 1974, p. 3.
[27] *Ibid.,* p. 4.

there has been a shift in Western thinking and policy.[28] While the Soviet Union always has been willing to follow the policy of peaceful coexistence, the West only recently developed a more "sober" and "realistic" attitude. This shift in Western policy has been caused, so this analysis goes, by the increasing crisis in the imperialist camp and the shifting power balance in favor of the Soviet Union. These factors have caused the West to be more cautious in its dealings with the Soviet Union and also have forced the United States to establish closer economic relations with the Soviet Union in order to compete more effectively with rival capitalist states.

Although the degree of enthusiasm for detente varies somewhat among Soviet analysts, they generally agree that it will further the interests of the Soviet Union and only temporarily aid capitalism. In the long run, the contradictions of the imperialist camp will be heightened. Because the Soviet Union will no longer appear to be threatening, for example, it will become increasingly difficult for the Western military-industrial complex to justify its rule and maintain the cohesion of its military alliances. In the meantime, the power of the Communist camp will grow, and there will be a gradual change in the global balance in favor of the Soviet Union.

For Moscow, then, peaceful coexistence is a form of class struggle and a method of weakening the capitalist states. Even the use of force is not completely ruled out against capitalist countries or even within the Socialist camp. Although Stalin's successors have allowed the possibility that nuclear war between the two systems may not be fatalistically "inevitable," and that states representing different social systems can coexist without recourse to general violence, Communists in the West have been warned that violence may be necessary in support of, or to protect, the revolution.

Apart from using detente to strengthen the Socialist camp economically, by obtaining credits, technology, and the like, the ideological

---

[28] For brief descriptions of Soviet views, see Walter Laqueur, *Detente, Western and Soviet Interpretations,* Strategic Studies Center, Stanford Research Institute, January 30, 1974; Foy Kohler, Mose Harvey, Leon Gouré, and Richard Soll, *Soviet Strategy for the Seventies, From Cold War to Peaceful Coexistence* (Miami: Center for Advanced International Studies, 1974); and Pipes, *op. cit.* On the evolution of the Soviet concept of "detente," see the monthly reports of Dimitri K. Simes, *Foreign Policy, Arms Control and Strategic Issues in the Soviet Media,* Georgetown University Center for Strategic and International Studies, 1975–77.

struggle is to be "intensified." This is not a trivial matter. It is not to be left only to the propagandists. Political and economic struggle in general is to be increased. There is to be peaceful coexistence between states, but not between social classes. The Soviet Union is to guard itself against Western efforts to take advantage of detente; and at the same time, the Soviet camp is to wage offensive ideological war.

The second major phenomenon of our time, as the Soviets call it, the general crisis of capitalism, has entered into a distinctive third phase. (The first phase was the period following the Bolshevik Revolution and the establishment of the world Communist movement, while the second took place in the 1930s and was highlighted by World War II). As Timour Timofeiev, Director of the USSR Academy of Sciences Institute of the International Workers Movement, observes, the third phase is "the crisis in the economic base of contemporary capitalism and the breakdown of the existing structure of the world's capitalist economic system, paralleled by a number of political, national, racial, and moral crises and drastic aggravation of social tension in the capitalist system as a whole. In other words, the intensifying general crisis of capitalism has become truly all-embracing."[29] "Never before have crisis processes in the economy, and the factors that deepen the political crisis in individual imperialist countries and in the whole system of capitalist international relations, been so closely interrelated, and never before have they so powerfully affected each other."[30]

The "crisis," the Soviets maintain, is manifest and can be seen in different areas—the energy crisis, economic policy crisis, overproduction crisis, and political-ideological crisis. It also can be seen in (a) relations within individual capitalist countries, which are said to be characterized by unemployment, together with rapid inflation and production stagnation (stagflation); (b) relations between the capitalist countries, such as US efforts to "exploit" its lead in oil and gas and "avenge" itself on the world market (symbolized by the collapse of the monetary system built on dollar supremacy), and the "counteroffensive" and "economic rivalry" of Western Europe and Japan; and (c) relations between the imperialist states and the Third World char-

---

[29] Timour Timofeiev, "The Banner of the Revolutionary Struggle of the Proletariat; On Trends in the Class Struggle Under the Conditions of the Aggravation of the General Crisis of Capitalism," *Kommunist,* April 1975.
[30] Ponomarev, *loc. cit.,* p. 8.

acterized by the "demands of the international monopolies for cheap raw materials and the response of the developing countries, which are asserting their sovereign right to dispose of the national wealth as they see fit."

This "crisis" also offers the Communists unprecedented opportunities to help shift the world balance of forces. As Timofeiev stated in the theoretical organ of the CPSU, Communists must observe "the pulsebeat of all political life and the state of the organized labor movement and the feelings of the broadest possible toiling masses. It is precisely on the basis of such an analysis that the Communists are drawing the conclusion as to their real possibility to implement an aggressive strategy in the class struggle in a number of links within the world's imperialist system."[31]

Timofeiev then goes on to describe the most important characteristics of the third phase of the capitalist crisis. First is the expansion of the scale of strikes in many capitalist countries. His figures indicate that in 1965 there were 36 million strikers in the entire capitalist world (19 million in the advanced capitalist countries). By 1974, the figures had risen to 65 million strikers, and 47 million in advanced capitalist countries. Second, the labor movement, to judge from its qualitatively new level of demands, has become increasingly aggressive. Apart from defending their daily interests, the workers are opposing "ever more frequently and adamantly the foundations of the economic and socio-political course of the ruling circles." Then there is the increasing internationalization of the class struggle. Working people are launching joint action not only within national frameworks but on an international scale as well. Among the most significant of these are (a) international coordination against multinational corporations; (b) the "strengthening of international solidarity" with Third World countries which wish to dispose of their wealth as they see fit; and (c) the "solution" to the complex problems of the migrant workers, and the incorporation and unification of the 12 to 20 million migrant workers in Europe into the struggle of the entire proletariat. Last, the processes contributing to the unification of a "broad front of popular forces" are developing quite rapidly. In the long run, these forces are related to the "scientific and technical revolution, and to the changes it has triggered in the social structure of society and the social structure of

---

[31] Timofeiev, *loc. cit.*

the working class, including the intensifying rapprochement between hired intellectual and manual labor."[32]

These changes in the capitalist social structure have been intensified by the economic crisis; and the results are especially apparent in France and Italy, where alliances between Communist and non-Communist groups are being forged in both political and trade union circles. This is part of a two-stage revolution—democratic first and Socialist later. It also can be seen in Portugal and Peru, where the "proletarian vanguard" has been able to make alliances with the military. In fact, Timofeiev states explicitly:[33]

> The progressive organizations, including the Communists, see in the solid alliance with progressive military personnel a prerequisite for the further development of the anti-Fascist and general democratic struggle, and the timely implementation of the changes that have ripened in society.

And he concludes his analysis of the resulting trends of the crisis:

> The developments in the 1970s in various parts of the capitalist world confirm the ripening of objective and subjective prerequisites needed for such a (revolutionary) change. The aggressive line of the Communist movement now stems from the need and increased real possibilities for an upsurge in the class struggle on a higher level.

In sum, the Soviets see the labor movement unified under Communist Party leadership as a highly useful means of weakening Western states and governments. Furthermore, their prospects for success have been enhanced by recent developments, such as the increased strength of the Communist camp, the consolidation of the principles of peaceful coexistence (detente), and the current or third stage of the general crisis of capitalism. In general, labor in the advanced capitalist states is more susceptible to this type of activity than in other regions; but the Soviets also seem to believe there are many opportunities in the Third World for the labor movement to be developed and unified under Communist leadership.

---

[32] *Ibid.*
[33] *Ibid.*

Specific Political-Military Usages

Yet the mechanisms by which the unified labor movement is to help shift the balance of forces in the direction of "socialism" have not been publicly specified by contemporary Soviet theoreticians. Nor have they discussed how labor can be used as an instrument of policy— except, of course, as part of the Soviet effort to promote "world revolution." Once again, past practice provides significant clues to Soviet thinking. Unless there has been a radical break with past practice, there are at least six specific usages of organized labor which can be considered part of the Soviet perspective. First, ever since the time of Lenin, Communists have referred to trade unions as "schools of communism." That is to say, the trade unions could be used to affect the attitudes of workers. After all, the unions are a significant part of a mass movement, and they have enormous potential. They have access to millions of workers on a daily basis, on docks, ships, planes, and loading platforms, and in factories, schools, and offices throughout the world. They can explain the bad times and the good times; they can identify the workers' "enemies" and point to the workers' "friends." When well managed, the organizational talent, muscle, and financial resources of the trade unions can be a potent propaganda tool, capable of guiding workers' attitudes and affecting their behavior in activities ranging from street demonstrations to elections.

Second, they know that trade unions, on occasion, can be used to infiltrate the government of a modern industrial state. Most advanced industrial societies have found it useful to include former union leaders in governmental bodies, and many high-ranking union officials serve on government, industrial, and economic commissions as nominees of their own movement. Communist Parties have been successful in placing former Communist trade union officials in senior and junior posts, particularly when they have been part of a governing coalition. This was a successful tactic in the nationalized industries of France and Italy following World War II.[34]

The use of political as opposed to the economic strikes is a third weapon the Soviet Union and Communist Parties have available. Economic strikes can be defined as those called to improve the wages

---

[34] Mario Einaudi, Maurice Bye, and Ernesto Rossi, *Nationalization in France and Italy* (Ithaca: Cornell University Press, 1951).

and working conditions of union members, simply and directly, although such strikes often have incidental political effects. For example, an increase in wages may lead to an inflationary spiral, which in a weak economic climate can create political repercussions and may undermine a government's popular standing. Economic strikes, however, are not called to create such political repercussions. They are unintended side effects, and unions will try to hold political fallout to a minimum in these circumstances.

A political strike, on the other hand, is not called to improve the lot of the workers, but rather to produce desired political consequences—inflation, instability, or the removal of uncooperative officials. It turns the strike weapon on its head. Improving the conditions of union members, if such should result from the political strike, is strictly incidental. In fact, the Soviets are contemptuous of strikes which serve "merely" to improve the lot of the workers and are not part of an overall political strategy. These are considered pure "economism"—reformist activities which temporarily ameliorate the conditions of the workers, but which in fact are part of bourgeois efforts to split the working class. In Allende's Chile, for example, strikers were criticized because they were "infected by ideas of economism (which) caused considerable harm to the Chilean revolution and served as one of the factors which weakened the popular unity government."[35]

Perhaps the most significant use of political strikes to promote Soviet objectives came in the post-World War II period. During the late 1940s, Moscow ordered the European Communist Parties to use political strikes to impede economic recovery, wreck the Marshall Plan, and undermine NATO and Western defense efforts. Both before and after that period, the Communists used political strikes in Europe and the Third World.[36]

In addition to using organized labor to support candidates, causes, and political strikes, the Soviets for many years have used labor for

---

[35] A. I. Sobolev, "Questions of Strategy and Tactics of the Class Struggle at the Present Stage of the General Crisis of Capitalism," *Rabochiy Klass I Sovremenny Mir*, FBIS, Soviet Union, February 19, 1975, p. A2.

[36] For a description of Communist political strikes against the Marshall Plan and NATO, see Roy Godson, *American Labor and European Politics, The AFL as a Transnational Force* (New York: Crane, Russak, 1976).

a variety of paramilitary activities. Obviously, information on these activities is very difficult to obtain. One of the most interesting confirmations of Soviet concern with the paramilitary uses of labor can be found in the writing of a former German Communist, Richard Krebs, who settled in the United States in 1940 after 20 years as a Communist organizer. In 1941 Krebs, under the pseudonym of Jan Valtin, published a sensational and flamboyant autobiography, *Out of the Night,* which became a best seller.[37] Krebs described his worldwide travels as a paid Communist organizer, his capture and torture by the Gestapo, and finally his escape from both the Gestapo and the Soviet secret police. Two thirds of the book, however, is devoted to describing Krebs' training and his organizing of trade unions for purposes of espionage, staging *coups d'état,* and creating paramilitary organizations to serve Russian ends.[38]

Soviet labor activities in Czechoslovakia in 1948 are an example of a *coup d'état* strategy that they may also have tried to implement in other countries, such as postwar France and Italy. Their main approach was to get control of labor in strategic industries—transportation, communications, electricity, and printing. Political strikes were then called either to bring down the government or to demonstrate that there could be no effective government unless Communists were included in it. The Communists then insisted on control of strategic ministries, preferably the police and the armed forces. While their demands were not met completely, they could insist at least that determined anti-Communists not control these sectors. Then, when it was judged auspicious actually to seize power, they used their control of labor organizations in key sectors to take over, or at least to impede the government's ability to maintain itself. In some circumstances, actions such as denying the government access to printing presses or the electronic media to mobilize people or transportation for the armed forces could be decisive.[39] Similarly, the trade unions could be very important in consolidating and maintaining power in the aftermath of a coup. The Bolsheviks did just that, and labor "fronts"

---

[37] Jan Valtin, *Out of the Night* (New York: Alliance, 1941).
[38] The US government also released a number of declassified or sanitized intelligence reports on Soviet efforts in this regard in the early postwar period. Some are reprinted in their entirety in Godson, *op. cit.,* Appendix C.
[39] On the attempted application of this tactic in France in 1947, see *ibid.*

modeled on this pattern have been established in almost all areas which Moscow-oriented Communists now control.[40]

The use of unions for espionage is also well known to the Kremlin. Apart from industrial espionage, sometimes unions can place workers in sensitive defense industries and installations. In postwar France, for example, Communist union officials in the CGT were convicted of spying on military activities in the docks. Ultimately, the French government had to cease employing CGT-"approved" workers in the maritime industry, and take security precautions at defense-related institutions in other parts of the country.[41]

Finally, the Soviets are well aware that trade unions have a variety of other paramilitary uses. During World War II, for example, the Allied governments used the unions for espionage, and also sabotage activities, in Nazi-occupied Europe.[42] After the war, the Soviets used Communist-controlled unions first in propaganda activities against rearmament,[43] and later to sabotage Western defense efforts. They also planned to use Communist-controlled trade unions as part of their underground apparatus in the event Communist Parties were banned or there was a war between the Soviet Union and the West. The postwar paramilitary use of labor was first reported by Western trade unionists who tried to neutralize these activities; and more recently, declassified CIA documents have helped to confirm these activities.[44]

Thus, organized labor has long been viewed by the Soviet leadership as a significant instrument of policy. The specific usages, of course, depended on their momentary objectives and expectations

---

[40] Jay B. Sorenson, *The Life and Death of Soviet Trade Unions, 1917–1928* (New York: Atherton, 1967); AFL Free Trade Union Committee, *What Happened to Trade Unions Behind the Iron Curtain* (1947); Paul Barton, *Conventions Collectives Et Réalités Ouvrières En Europe De L'Est* (Paris: Editions Ouvrières, 1957); Force Ouvrière, *Les Ouvrières Face A La Dictature, 1938–1968* (Paris: Confédération Force Ouvrière, 1969).

[41] Godson, *op. cit.*

[42] Very little has been written about this, and it is impossible to obtain access to OSS Labor Division files. For a brief discussion of the OSS Labor Division, see *ibid.*, especially Appendix A. For a description of Communist labor activities in the Resistance, see the Communist CGT leader Andre Tollet's *La Classe Ouvrière Dans la Résistance* (Paris: Editions Sociales, 1969).

[43] William Douglas, "West German Communism As an Aid to Moscow," *World Affairs,* March 1970; and Godson, *op. cit.*

[44] See Godson, *op. cit.*, especially Appendix C.

about what could be acomplished. Unless their thinking about labor
is simply rhetoric, or they have concluded that their past activities
have been mistaken, misdirected, or simply would not be effective today, these perspectives should provide a reasonable guide to future
attempts to use labor throughout the world.

2

Labor As An Instrument of Soviet National Security Policy

Soviet behavior in the international labor movement is, of course, tied to Soviet national security policy. The Soviet leadership coordinates a vast array of overt and covert institutions based in the USSR, Eastern Europe, Cuba, and other parts of the world in an effort to gain control of a significant sector in the non-Communist world.

Policymaking and Implementation

The Politburo of the CPSU is the key policymaking body of the Soviet Union. It determines Soviet objectives and orchestrates the instrumentalities. Tracing the formulation and implementation of Politburo policy with respect to organized labor, however, is no easy matter. From time to time, the Kremlin releases information on foreign-oriented labor activities, but several institutions which deal with labor matters are rarely discussed publicly. For example, the activities of Soviet intelligence agencies, which have been concerned with organized labor since the Bolshevik seizure of power, are seldom exposed to public gaze—at least deliberately. Almost certainly, however, the Politburo in one way or another takes into account and coordinates KGB programs with AUCCTU activities. Similarly, the Central Committee Secretariat, the Ministry of Foreign Affairs, research institutes, and possibly the GRU (Soviet military intelligence)[45] are also involved in developing and executing Politburo decisions.

There are indications that several key officials have major responsibilities for policymaking with respect to labor. Certainly one must be M. Suslov, who is one of the three senior Party Secretaries, and the man who usually chairs the weekly Politburo meetings in Brezhnev's absence. He has overall responsibilities for ideology, and for relations with ruling and nonruling Communist Parties and other institutions of the working class. A. Kirilenko, another senior CPSU Secretary and senior Politburo member, has responsibility for overall coordination of Politburo and Party affairs. A third leading figure is Boris Ponomarev. He is a candidate member of the Politburo, one of seven CPSU Secretaries and head of the Central Committee's International Department. As the Politburo does not have its own staff, apart from Brezhnev's personal assistants, it is likely that this department, like other Central Committee departments, services the Politburo on these matters.

There are 80 to 100 professional staff in Ponomarev's department, subdivided into "desks" that, in addition to dealing with nonruling Communist Parties, also are concerned with non-Communist, but Socialist-oriented parties and nongovernmental organizations. The Department, in turn, also appears to be serviced by a number of research centers belonging to the Social Sciences Section of the Praesidium of the USSR Academy of Sciences, such as the well-known Institute of World Economics and International Relations (IMEMO), the Institute for the Study of the USA and Canada (IUSAC), and the less well-known Institute of the International Workers Movement (IMRD). There are also institutes dealing with Africa, Latin America, and the Far East.[46]

---

[45] Presumably, the GRU is responsible for intelligence about Western military bases and defense production and transportation. This information can be obtained from the military who may be unionized, but also, as was discussed in Part One, from civilians and union officials working on the bases or employed in military production and transportation.

[46] For a discussion of the role of foreign policy analysts in Soviet decisionmaking, see Oded Eran, *The "Mezhdunarodniki," Soviet Foreign Experts* (forthcoming), and Richard S. Soll, Arthur A. Zuelke, Jr., and Richard B. Foster, *The Role of Social Science Research Institutes in the Formulation and Execution of Soviet Foreign Policy,* Stanford Research Institute, Strategic Studies Center, March 1976, especially pp. 13–40.

Some of the work of these institutes has been coordinated within the context of socalled Scientific Councils of Complex Problems in order to avoid duplication in overlapping subject matter, and to yield a multidisciplinary output on a given problem. In 1961, for example, a Scientific Council on the Complex Problems of Economic Competition of the Two Systems was established; and a few years later, a Council on the Complex Problems of Working Class and Democratic Mass Movements in Capitalist Countries was created. Together, they publish an irregular "annual" serial, *Competition of the Two Systems*. The editorial board of this journal consists of A. M. Rumyantsev (formerly a member of the Central Committee), D. M. Gvishiani (Deputy Chairman of the State Committee for Science and Technology), G. A. Arbatov (Director of IUSAC), and N. N. Inosemtsev (Director of IMEMO), both candidate members of the Central Committee, the Directors of the Institutes of Far East and African Studies, and Timour Timofeiev, Director of the Institute of the International Workers Movement (IMRD).

The IMRD focuses almost exclusively on labor, and particularly international labor affairs. Unlike IUSAC and IMEMO and the other institutes mentioned above, which are placed in the Economics Department of the Social Science Division, the IMRD—until recently, at least—was independently attached to the Social Science Division. Timofeiev, son of the American Communist Eugene Dennis, reportedly is on good personal terms with Suslov and Ponomarev. The departments of the Institute conduct research in specific problem areas, such as complex theoretical problems of the world revolutionary process; the workers movement in the developed capitalist countries; social and economic positions of the workers; international organizations; trade union movements; and contemporary history and international problems of the workers movement.[47] Very few of the publications of this high-ranking and well-placed institute have been reviewed by Western scholars, and little is known in the United States about its work.

In the AUCCTU itself, there are probably two key officials. One is Piotr Pimenov, a 63-year-old AUCCTU Praesidium Secretary, who

---

[47] O. N. Melikyan, "The Activity of the Institute of the International Workers Movement of the Academy of Sciences of the USSR: Structure, Basic Directions of Research Works," *Competition of the Two Systems* (Moscow: Nauka, 1970), pp. 452–457.

is a member of the CPSU Central Committee as well. Even before the 1975 demise of Politburo member Aleksandr Shelepin, who was also Chairman of the AUCCTU Praesidium, Pimenov was regarded as the key professional and the Number Two man. A former engineer who has spent most of his career in "trade union" work, Pimenov also has had considerable experience in international labor affairs. He was a Secretary of the Soviet-controlled World Federation of Trade Unions in Prague in the early 1960s; he has attended numerous international labor gatherings; and currently he is an elected worker member of the ILO Governing Body.

The second official is 62-year-old Aleksei Shibaev, who was appointed to Shelepin's post as Chairman of the AUCCTU Praesidium in November 1976. Shibaev, however, like most AUCCTU Chairmen, has had no previous labor experience. He was trained as an engineer, served as a plant manager in Gorky, and was appointed a provincial Party Secretary in 1959 and a member of the CPSU Central Committee in 1961. Unlike previous AUCCTU chairmen, and particularly Shelepin, Shibaev is not an important political figure. Moreover, given his background he presumably knows little about the international labor movement. Probably it will take years before he becomes fully proficient in his new job, especially with regard to the labor movement in the non-Communist world. Thus it is difficult to imagine that he will overshadow Pimenov for some time to come, in substance at least. In sum, although senior KGB and other officials are probably also involved, there seems little doubt that Suslov, Kirilenko, and Ponemarev, with input from Timofeiev, Pimenov, and in future Shibaev, are responsible for developing Soviet policy in the international labor movement.

Apart from the KGB, the Ministry of Foreign Affairs, and similar organizations, the main policy implementing institution is AUCCTU. The AUCCTU is completely controlled by the Politburo, and—as was pointed out in Part One—the national labor center insists that it unswervingly follows the Party's directives.[48] Just how the AUCCTU decides on methods of implementation is not at all clear. Edwin Morrell has pointed out that, in contrast to other subject matter in

---

[48] On CPSU control of AUCCTU, see Edwin Morrell, *Communist Unionism, Organized Labor and the Soviet State* (unpublished Ph.D. thesis, Harvard University, 1965); Thomas Lowit, *Le Syndicalisme de Type Sovietique* (Paris: Armand Colin, 1971).

which the AUCCTU Praesidium and Secretariat have implemented Politburo directives, foreign policy decisions appear to be made outside the usual channels. There appears to be almost no discussion of them in plenums, and they are not discussed in either the bulletins or "protocol" pamphlets of the Praesidium or the Secretariat. Conceivably, the AUCCTU Praesidium and Secretariat have been making the decisions, but they have been restrictively classified and not distributed through the normal, but already restrictively distributed, bulletins and "protocol" pamphlets.[49] Or possibly the key decisions on implementation are being taken elsewhere, perhaps in the Communist Party Secretariat and/or the intelligence services.

In any event, within AUCCTU there is a major department concerned with implementing Politburo directives. The International Affairs Department is one of the largest in AUCCTU. It has a professional staff of about 100 divided along geographical, and to some extent functional, lines.[50] There are specialists divided into a number of sections, including (a) Western Capitalist States, (b) Middle East and Africa, (c) Asia, (d) Latin America and the Caribbean, and (e) International Organizations. There are also international affairs "advisors" both to the AUCCTU Secretariat and to the International Affairs Department. For example, the current head of the International Affairs Department was listed only as an advisor until he became Director in 1975.

In addition to the International Affairs Department, a number of other departments have two or three specialists concerned with foreign relations. Many industrial departments—for example, the agricultural workers—have specialists concerned with foreign unions in their industries. (A few American unions also have one or two international affairs specialists.) The Higher Trade Union School also has a Research Section with four or five foreign affairs specialists. This school, which now is housed in one of the best buildings in Moscow, employs a number of specialists to teach foreign trade unionists selected to study in Moscow. (Since 1961, about 3,300 foreign unionists from 75 countries have studied there, and about 1,000 have received a diploma as a result of completing the ten-month

---

[49] Morrell, *op. cit.*, pp. 522–535.
[50] By way of contrast, the AFL-CIO International Affairs Department has a professional staff of nine.

course.[51]) In addition, it should be noted that there is also a completely separate AUCCTU department, with a staff of seven to ten professionals, concerned with the labor organizations of ruling Communist Parties. The Higher Trade Union School also has another special faculty for students from these countries. Over the past three years, over 1,300 "trade unionists" from Soviet bloc countries have apparently attended this school.[52]

To implement policy, Moscow also can call on labor and political institutions in Eastern Europe and Cuba, the World Federation of Trade Unions (WFTU) in Prague, and Moscow-oriented Communist Parties, particularly in Europe. While there may be differences on some subjects between the East European and Cuban Communist leadership on one hand and the Soviet leadership on the other, there are few discernible differences in labor-related activities among these Moscow-oriented Communist Parties. In policy, in votes at international labor forums, and in general activities, the Soviets, East Europeans, and Cubans appear to be engaged in almost identical pursuits. This provides the Kremlin with literally hundreds of additional international labor professionals, and numerous channels for training, influencing, and supporting foreign union leaders.

For example, in addition to AUCCTU's Higher Trade Union School for foreign trade unionists referred to above, over half a dozen training centers for foreign union leaders have been established in Eastern Europe since World War II. Although information on the centers is hard to come by, the three major centers are the International Trade Union School in Prague, the Fritz Heckert Institute in Bernau, East Germany, and the George Dimitrov Center in Sofia. At the Bulgarian center alone, over 1,800 trade union functionaries from 60 countries have passed through the ten-month and shorter courses and seminars. (The Bulgarian trade union newspaper *Trud* pointed to this training of labor cadres from Latin America, Africa, and Asia as an "extremely important manifestation of international and class solidarity."[53]) In January 1976, the Cubans opened the Lazaro Pena

[51] J. Svetlicnij, "At Moscow, A University for Trade Unionists from All Over the World," *World Trade Union Movement,* October 1976, pp. 30–31; and *Flashes,* September 10, 1975. *World Trade Union Movement* is a monthly, and *Flashes* a biweekly, publication of the WFTU.
[52] *Flashes,* October 13, 1976.
[53] BTA (Bulgarian News Agency), February 13, 1976.

national trade union school. It already has run two international courses for Latin Americans and Cubans. The second course, which lasted for three months, was also attended by 50 "Angolan trade unionists."[54]

Just how the Soviets coordinate their programs with their allies is uncertain. Like AUCCTU, the East European "trade unions" have active international affairs departments and sizeable staffs. There are periodic meetings of representatives of these bodies with their Soviet counterparts at Warsaw Pact and CEMA meetings, as well as at special meetings.[55] They also caucus at international labor gatherings. But perhaps the greatest number of contacts takes place at bilateral meetings between Soviet labor officials and representatives from individual bloc countries. Indeed, there is almost constant contact and interchange at every level. No doubt these meetings also serve ritualistic purposes, but they are undoubtedly used to discuss substantive matters as well.

In spite of their differences with some nonruling Communist Parties, the Soviets also cooperate closely with a number of them in the labor field. Certainly in the past, the Italians were a major vehicle for Soviet activities in Africa; and today, the French Communist Party and CGT are cooperating directly with the Soviets and the WFTU.[56]

The World Federation of Trade Unions

The WFTU is the most important Soviet-controlled international labor body. Essentially, it was created in 1945 to serve Soviet purposes after World War II and the eclipse of most of the interwar international labor centers. Most probably, it will continue to exist until the Soviets decide it is no longer useful.

With the exception of the AFL, almost all significant Communist and non-Communist national centers joined in the immediate postwar period. The Western international trade secretariats, however,

---

[54] *Flashes,* October 13, 1976.
[55] For a recent report on a "consultative meeting of national centers of the Socialist countries and the WFTU," see *ibid.*
[56] In Spring 1977, for example, the WFTU and the CGT center for aid to trade unions in the developing countries signed a cooperative agreement. The CGT, together with the WFTU and Soviet and East European centers, were also applauded by a number of Communist unions in Latin America and the Caribbean for their assistance at a meeting in Havana, Cuba. *Ibid.,* May 4 and May 27, 1977.

also refused to become affiliated. (Unions in a given industry—transport workers, for example—can join these industry-oriented international labor bodies called international trade secretariats, hereafter referred to as ITS.) Together with the AFL, their leaders believed that the WFTU was Soviet-controlled and would be used to support Moscow's political objectives. After the Kremlin tried to use the WFTU to disrupt the Marshall Plan and Western defense efforts, the non-Communist Western centers withdrew in 1949 and joined with the AFL in creating the International Confederation of Free Trade Unions (ICFTU), abandoning the WFTU to Soviet dominance.[57] Since then, although Moscow has occasionally experienced some slight difficulties controlling the organization, particularly in the aftermath of the Soviet invasion of Czechoslovakia, the WFTU has generally served Soviet interests.

The WFTU claims to be the largest, and therefore the most representative, international labor federation. But while the WFTU claims that its affiliates have over 160 million individual members, it should be noted that almost all of this membership is derived from Communist countries (over half from the Soviet Union alone), where union membership is almost a necessity of life. The membership figures from 20 to 30 non-Communist countries, which comprise five to ten percent of the WFTU affiliation, are very difficult to verify and almost certainly exaggerated. Under these circumstances, membership figures are not very significant; and outside of the Communist bloc, India, France, and Italy, the WFTU is relatively small—approximately five percent of workers affiliated with trade unions.

The WFTU also has created eleven international industrial labor bodies, or trade union internationals (TUIs), constituted from national unions affiliated to the WFTU, which are the WFTU's counterparts to the previously mentioned ITS. But unlike the ITS, they are funded by and subordinate to the WFTU's governing bodies. They present to the Kremlin another vehicle to influence industrial unions not affiliated with the WFTU.

The internal government of the WFTU may correspond to the standard pattern for international labor federations—a quadrennial

---

[57] For detailed analysis of this early postwar period, see Godson, *op. cit.;* and Morton Schwartz, *Soviet Policies in the WFTU* (unpublished Ph.D. thesis, Columbia University, 1963).

Congress, a 34- to 35-member Executive Bureau and a 72-member General Council; but in reality, the locus of power lies elsewhere. The WFTU's archives are not open to Western scholars; but it would appear that currently, the key policymakers within the organization are the President, three Vice Presidents, and the Secretariat, composed of a General Secretary and five Secretaries. Although the men who hold these positions represent various countries and continents (the President is Uruguayan, the Vice Presidents Indian, Dahomean, and Czech, the General Secretary French, and the Secretaries Soviet, Cypriot, Chilean, Indian, and Sudanese), the Kremlin appears to control the organization completely.

To be sure, the Soviets have had difficulties from time to time persuading all the affiliates and the Secretariat of the "correctness" of Soviet policy and the Soviet concept of the organization. The Italian CGIL, for example, as well as leading members of the Secretariat based at the headquarters in Prague, were clearly opposed to the invasion of Czechoslovakia. The Italian Communists in the late 1960s, for their own tactical political reasons, also wanted the organization to become involved in nonpolitical trade union affairs. Indeed, the Italian Secretary proposed using the TUIs, especially their East and West European affiliates, for this very purpose. The Soviets reportedly were unhappy with this nonpolitical approach, and were especially upset at the prospect of Soviet and East European labor officials meeting as a group to discuss such questions as differences in wages and working conditions and the problems of workers in the Communist bloc.

In spite of these occasional difficulties, however, the Soviets almost always have managed to have their way. Why? First, they are usually very well informed about developments within the organization. Soviet citizens are assigned to all major departments, and key officials are often Soviet citizens, or their deputies are. (In 1975, for example, a very experienced labor operator, Boris Averyanov, who headed the AUCCTU's Department of International Affairs for a number of years, was appointed a WFTU Secretary.) Second, as will be discussed below, the Soviets reportedly provide the organization with almost all its funds. Indeed, according to a former high-ranking WFTU official, when Western affiliates complained that the disproportionately high number of Soviet and East European officials were unable to work effectively in Western countries, because they did not understand such things as collective bargaining, the Soviets responded that if the Western affiliates were dissatisfied they should pay for their own staff. Third, the Soviets and their allies, comprising well over half of the WFTU's affiliated membership, control enough votes to settle any issue in their favor. Usually, however, they prefer not to risk divisive votes at international meetings. Instead, they consult with, and if necessary pressure, affiliates prior to formal meetings to ensure their policies are adopted without division. In the event that an affiliate is still reluctant to go along, CPSU officials sometimes will pressure the affiliate's parent Communist Party to ensure compliance.

By virtue of the fact that they are well informed and have the votes, the funds, and leverage in the international Communist movement, the Soviets have almost always managed to retain their control. When necessary, recalcitrant officials have been removed, and the WFTU has always fallen into line with basic Soviet policy on issues where initially there was disagreement, such as the Marshall Plan, the "expulsion" of the Chinese, and the European Economic Community.

To implement its decisions, the WFTU has a professional staff of over 200 officials in Prague, and several representatives in various parts of the world. (Ernest de Maio, until recently Vice President of the Communist-controlled American union, the United Electrical Workers, was appointed in 1975 to represent the WFTU at the UN headquarters in New York.) There are departments dealing with economic and social affairs, TUIs, publications, education, and international organizations. A new department to coordinate activities relating to multinational corporations was created recently; and in 1974, a committee of international labor scholars from nine member countries was established under the direction of Professor Baglai of Timofeiev's Institute on the International Workers Movement. The major function of the committee, according to Baglai, is to coordinate research on economic and social trends that relate to the international labor movement, as well as to bring social scientists of "the most different tendencies" into contact with each other.[58]

The WFTU's main activities are serving as a propaganda agency, promoting trade union unity, providing political training to non-Western union leaders, and financially supporting favored unions.

---

[58] *World Trade Union Movement,* March 1976, pp. 13–15.

The organization engages in very few strictly trade union activities. It is basically politically oriented, although during the past few years it has shown more interest in economic and social affairs. Disseminating propaganda is one of its most important purposes, and the main targets are workers and union officials in the non-Communist world. A number of themes can be found in its monthly magazine *World Trade Union Movement,* which is translated into nine languages and disseminated throughout the world, as well as in the numerous propaganda conferences held in Europe and the non-Western world. Apart from stressing the achievements of the Communist states (it maintains there are many) and the role of their unions (which, it says, have few, if any, problems) the organization's main emphasis is on the need for the worldwide unification of the labor movement.

The WFTU stresses that the "Socialist" states, their labor organizations, and the WFTU affiliates in the non-Communist world are against all things that men fear most: economic insecurity, social injustice, exploitation, militarism, and war. This theme is adapted to fit in with the issues of the day and the particular geographical region. It is designed to appeal to workers and union officials for whom opposition to global and regional evils is a worthwhile objective, regardless of who is promoting it. This often effectively blurs the distinction between Communist and non-Communist union leaders. After all, if the Communists support such worthy goals, why should not Communists as well as non-Communists work and join together? Why should not trade unions throughout the world unite to promote these common aims? Or so the propaganda goes.

Another major tactic of the WFTU's propaganda apparatus is to capitalize on interest clashes between the socalled Third World and the West. Reacting to Suez in 1956, the Congo in 1961, the overthrow of Allende's regime in Chile, apartheid in South Africa, and the Arab-Israeli conflict, the WFTU is quick to side with the position of Third World governments against, for the most part, that of Western countries. On the basis of these "common positions" and solidarity with the governments and the unions of the developing countries, the Soviets attempt to produce attitudes and consequences favorable to the Soviet bloc and damaging to the Western powers.

To further the momentum generated by its propaganda, the WFTU also promotes joint actions and other measures to "unify" Communist and non-Communist labor organizations on the international and re-

gional levels, and to weaken and disintegrate the ICFTU and its
regional organizations. Since the split in the international labor movement in the late 1940s and the creation of the democratic, Western-
oriented ICFTU, the WFTU has continuously proposed to the ICFTU
and the democratic Christian-oriented World Confederation of Labor
(WCL) and their affiliates that "unity of action" would vastly increase the strength of the labor movement. (Organic unity of non-
Communist and non-Communist international organizations is a long-
range goal.) A WFTU General Council meeting reiterated this
point for the hundredth time. Noting that "encouraging results"
have been achieved in bringing together national unions with different ideological affiliations, and that there has been progress in bringing about cooperation between the WFTU, the ICFTU, and WCL,
the resolution stated that these results were still insufficient to bring
the struggle of the workers to the level of present demands.[59]

> The WFTU considers that ideological differences do not present
> insurmountable obstacles; and that it is possible, while respect-
> ing each other's positions, to find ways toward an understanding
> which could lead to the creation of an international trade union
> center, grouping all the world's trade unions.

The WFTU also frequently calls on the ICFTU and the WCL to
join with it in supporting specific propaganda projects, such as the
"defense of democracy in Portugal," support for the "antiapartheid"
movement, and "justice for Palestinians," almost any project that
would lead non-Communist unions away from working solely through
the ICFTU and WCL.[60]

The WFTU, unlike the ICFTU, was reluctant from its inception
to sponsor regional organizations, perhaps because of what one writer
has called the "efficiency of centralized administration" under Soviet
direction, and because it feared losing control.[61] Unencumbered by
a regional structure (perhaps with the exception of CPUSTAL, dis-

---

[59] *Ibid.*, November 1975, p. 12.
[60] On the relative success of the Soviets and the WFTU in their efforts to unify
the three international centers, see John P. Windmuller, "Realignment In The
I.C.F.T.U.: The Impact of Detente," *British Journal of Industrial Relations,*
1976, pp. 247–260.
[61] John P. Windmuller, *Labor Internationals,* New York State School of Industrial and Labor Relations, Cornell University, 1969, p. 37.

cussed below), however, the WFTU has had little difficulty entering into frequently cooperative relations with several autonomous regional trade union bodies in the non-Western world.

During the 1950s and 1960s, several of these regional bodies sprang up in African and Asian countries which wanted to project their ambitions and nationalism into the international labor movement. Declaring a desire to be independent from the three major international labor bodies, they encouraged their affiliates to withdraw from the global internationals, which in fact meant withdrawal from the ICFTU, as very few non-Western movements had been attached to the WFTU.

The WFTU, of course, encouraged this "anti-imperialist" move, and entered into friendly and cooperative relations with these bodies. The first was the International Confederation of Arab Trade Unions (ICATU). Founded with the professed aim of furthering pan-Arab unity, as well as economic and social development, in 1956, the organization was created by and still remains basically under the control of the Egyptian government. The requirements of "unity" and "economic and social advancement" are by and large determined by the Egyptians, although trade union bodies from 16 Arab countries are now affiliated to ICATU.[62] The relationship between ICATU and the WFTU is, of course, partly a function of Egyptian-Soviet relations. Over the past 20 years, there have been fluctuations; but in spite of Sadat's current differences with the Soviet leadership, the ties between ICATU and the WFTU remain friendly. In 1969, for example, a WFTU-ICATU Standing Working Committee was created to coordinate "joint and similar activities"; and in the past four years, the WFTU feels that cooperative relations have "developed continuously."[63]

The Standing Committee, which meets periodically to plan joint educational and propaganda activities, serves to enhance the influence

---

[62] It should be noted, however, that in recent years about half of ICATU's affiliates, the "trade unions" in Iraq, Syria, North Yemen, South Yemen, Kuwait, and the PLO labor organizations, have also become members of the WFTU.
[63] See the report on the Sixth ICATU Congress in *World Trade Union Movement,* May 1976, p. 20. For a discussion of the origin and early relationship between ICATU and the WFTU, see Willard A. Beiling, *Pan-Arabism and Labor* (Cambridge: Harvard University Press, 1960). See also George E. Lichtblau, "The Communist Labor Offensive in Former Colonial Countries," *Industrial and Labor Relations Review,* April 1961, pp. 376–401.

of the WFTU, and hence of the Soviets in the Arab world. In these forums and in periodicals, the vestiges of colonialism and neoimperialism, especially "Zionism," are castigated. The WFTU also attacks "reactionary" Arab regimes which it maintains are repressing trade union rights, such as in Bahrein, Saudi Arabia, the United Arab Emirates, Jordan; and also Iran.

Another organization used by the Soviets and the WFTU was the All-African Trade Union Federation (AATUF). Created in 1961 by the more "radical" labor figures in Africa (the Casablanca group), this organization, like ICATU, supported regional "unity," denounced imperialism, colonialism, and so forth, and basically reflected the approach of the radical nationalist regimes and especially of one country, Nkrumah's Ghana. From its founding until the overthrow of Nkrumah in 1966, the organization's headquarters were in Accra; its Secretary General was a Ghanaian, and the bulk of its funds came from Nkrumah's "contingency funds." Although AATUF officially was unaligned, it worked closely with the WFTU and AUCCTU, overtly and covertly. Original letters and documents published by the Ghanaian unions after the fall of NKrumah not only demonstrate the way in which he manipulated the organization to subvert what he regarded as hostile (pro-Western) foreign trade unions and governments, but also the form and even the covert techniques that were used by the Soviet bloc to support the organization.[64]

Although the Soviets had for some reason cut down their subsidy to AATUF even before the fall of Nkrumah, the organization deteriorated in the late 1960s; and during the past year or two, most African trade union centers have joined the Organization of African Trade Union Unity (OATUU), formed under the aegis of the government-level Organization of African Unity in 1973. The WFTU at first maintained that the new organization was a tool of "the imperialists and their reformist vassals" to prevent trade union unity on the African continent. But in the Spring of 1975, WFTU's attitude changed; and in August 1976, a WFTU delegation visited the OATUU Sec-

---

[64] See B.A. Bentum, *Trade Unions in Chains: How Kwame Nkrumah destroyed free trade unions in Ghana and attempted to extend this on the African continent,* Trade Union Congress of Ghana, Accra, December 1966. See also G. E. Lynd, *The Politics of African Trade Unionism* (New York: Praeger, 1968), pp. 163–171. Lynd is the pseudonym of George Lichtblau, who for a number of years was the State Department's intelligence expert on the international labor movement.

retariat in Accra and signed an agreement "establishing practical cooperation between the two organizations."[65]

In Latin America, the situation is a little different. Reflecting a different history and stage of development, many of the unions in the region have been affiliated loosely with one of the regional bodies of the three global internationals, ICFTU, WCL, and WFTU. The Soviet bloc's current regional body, the Permanent Committee for Labor Unity in Latin America (CPUSTAL), which is nominally independent of the bloc and WFTU, however, has had a very difficult time surviving as an organization. Founded in Brazil in 1964, the organization originally established its headquarters in Chile. But since the Pinochet coup, CPUSTAL has not even had a home, and it does not want to be marked too easily by basing itself in Cuba. More and more in recent years, small Communist unions in Latin America have been affiliated directly with the WFTU, while at the same time attempting to unify with the larger non-Communist trade union bodies on the national and regional level.

In Asia, where a large number of Communist Parties have tried to stay neutral in the Sino-Soviet struggle, the WFTU has not been able to attach itself to any regional trade union body, and few Asian unions have affiliated directly to it. (The Chinese have not been formally expelled from the WFTU, but for all practical purposes they have not been members since the mid-1960s.) But WFTU officials have stepped up their efforts at building a regional trade union body in the area.[66]

The WFTU is also used to train labor cadres throughout the world. While the Soviets and the East Europeans frequently have bilateral relationships, and bring non-Western "trade unionists" to the Soviet Union and Eastern Europe for training, the WFTU is often used to select foreigners for training where it would be politically unwise for the Soviets to be involved directly. The WFTU also conducts regional training programs in cooperation with either a regional labor body or a sympathetic trade union center.

In Arab or African countries, for example, an AUCCTU or Soviet Foreign Ministry or KGB official will select what they regard as

---

[65] *World Trade Union Movement,* August 1975, pp. 8–9; and *ibid.,* September 1976, pp. 8–9.
[66] On the WFTU's analysis of trends in the region and efforts at organizing a regional body, see *ibid.,* January 1977, pp. 14, 17.

promising union officials and offer them scholarships at one of the Soviet or East European schools. If, however, individuals in a given country might find it politically uncomfortable to accept (perhaps because their government does not want too many people attending training programs in the Soviet Union), the WFTU could issue the invitation, or the WFTU could run a training program in the region, so that the local leaders would not have to travel to the Soviet Union.

Usually, the training—whether conducted in a Soviet-bloc school or at a regional seminar—is almost completely ideological and political. Unlike the foreign labor education projects of the AFL-CIO, for example, little or no attention is devoted to the rudiments of organizing, negotiation, collective bargaining, and grievance procedures —the basic bread and butter concerns of unionists. Rather, they are designed to improve the propaganda skills and orientation, as opposed to the technical skills, of the student. Based on the reports of former instructors and students in these schools, a three- or ten-month course in the Soviet Union would include several months of Russian language and literature, Soviet history, "political economy," philosophy, and "scientific communism," the history of the international labor movement, and bookkeeping.[67]

A somewhat similar curriculum (with perhaps less emphasis on the Soviet Union and without language training) is taught at regional WFTU schools. Usually, the program will also be tailored to apply to the particular region or industry, especially if it is conducted under the auspices of a TUI or a particular WFTU Department. These seminars are organized in one or more parts of the world almost on a monthly basis. For example, a report on a four-day textile industry seminar in Quito, Ecuador, organized by the Textile TUI with the collaboration of the Communist-oriented Ecuador Confederation of Labor, and with the participation of CPUSTAL, the ILO, and a fraternal delegation of AUCCTU textile workers, stated that 62 delegates from ten Latin American countries attended. After discussing the working environment of textile, clothing, leather, fur, and shoe workers, and the implementation of ILO conventions on freedom of asso-

---

[67] Interviews with former AUCCTU instructors who have emigrated, and interviews with former Moroccan, Egyptian, and Palestinian "students" in the Soviet Union and Eastern Europe. A brief history and description of these activities can also be found in *Afro-Asian Labor Bulletin,* March 1972, published by the National Trade Union Congress of Singapore.

ciation, "the participants noted that in all Latin American countries, except the Socialist Republic of Cuba, the working environment was harmful to workers' health and some cases unsuitable for human beings, which in addition to exploitation by imperialism and monopolism, daily worsened their working conditions."[68] Another report noted that the WFTU and the Fiji Council of Trade Unions organized a seminar attended by 32 representatives from five trade union organizations of different affiliations or independent, from Fiji, Australia, New Caledonia, and East Timor. The main topic was "Labor Versus Capital." "Various lecturers gave courses on the role of trade unions, the multinational companies, the international trade movement, and unity."[69]

Based on figures supplied by the Soviets and East Europeans as well as the WFTU, approximately 2,000 trade union officials from non-Western countries now attend courses from three to ten months duration each year,[70] and approximately the same number attend regional seminars usually sponsored by the WFTU and lasting from several days to two weeks. The Soviets began these sizeable training programs more modestly in the late 1960s, and have increased them in recent years. It would appear that approximately 15,000 non-Western officials have attended courses in the Soviet Union and Eastern Europe, and another 10,000 to 15,000 participated in the much shorter programs in their own region. As far as can be determined, however, these training programs are not used directly to train local leaders in how to conduct political strikes, engage in espionage, or in *coups d'état*. But it is quite possible that these educational activities may be used to identify cadres for this special type of training, or as a method of providing cover for an individual who undergoes such training.

A fourth technique used by the WFTU is financing foreign trade unions. Very little information is available on these matters. The Soviets and the WFTU do not usually publish financial statements. Moreover, according to a former high-ranking WFTU official, a small committee comprised of Soviet officials and the General Secretary

---

[68] *Flashes*, September 3, 1976.
[69] *Ibid.*, September 24, 1976. For reports on WFTU training programs in Africa, see *ibid.*, September 10, 1976.
[70] See, for example, *ibid.*, December 7, 1976.

meet in private to allocate these funds. Based on a few pieces of information and some reasonable calculations, however, it is possible to draw some conclusions about the organization's financing of foreigners. One of the best indications of WFTU activities in this area came in the 1960s. Cornell Professor John P. Windmuller published "hard" data which indicated that the WFTU had an International Solidarity Fund that spent $1.3 million during a 40-month period between January 1, 1962, and June 30, 1965. A breakdown of this annual budget of approximately $325,000 indicated that 60 percent went into trade union support in non-Western areas; 25 percent was spent in support of "national liberation" struggles; and about 15 percent went to support strikes and other forms of conflict in unspecified areas.[71]

Although, as Professor Windmuller and others have pointed out, the WFTU appeared to suffer from a major shortage of funds in the mid-1960s, this no longer appears to be true, judging from the increased rate of its publications and activities, and some recent figures published by the WFTU. At the General Council meeting in October 1975, a WFTU Secretary, according to conference documents, made a financial report and discussed the draft budget for 1976. He stated that the WFTU had received nearly $1 million for the International Solidarity Fund. This would be almost three times the annual expenditure of the fund a decade earlier. About $200,000 had been spent on "the struggle against imperialism, colonialism, and the monopolies"; and in view of "the crisis of capitalism," this was to be increased to $300,000 in 1976. Unfortunately, more comprehensive figures are not available, but there are also occasional reports of WFTU grants to trade unions in various countries.[72] In addition, because many of the small Communist-run national centers in Latin America and Africa receive almost no money in dues, it is not unreasonable to conclude that they are receiving a major portion of their limited funds in subsidies from the Soviet bloc and the WFTU. Otherwise, it is difficult to see how they could survive on an operational basis, let alone send representatives to international meetings.

The WFTU also has some potential use as a vehicle for promoting or coordinating political strikes. In the late 1940s, the Russians tried

---

[71] Windmuller, *Labor Internationals,* pp. 35–36.
[72] For example, the *Nigerian Herald* of April 23, 1976, reported that the WFTU had given the Nigerian TUC $30,000.

to use the organization in conjunction with European Communist Parties to run political strikes against the Marshall Plan and Western defense efforts. By and large, this effort failed, largely due to the transnational coalition of non-Communist European and American trade unionists and Western governments.[73] Since that time, the WFTU and the TUIs have occasionally tried to organize or join in international political strikes or boycotts. Usually these efforts have failed, mainly because non-Communist union leaders refused to take part in activities such as national political strikes, and particularly in international political strikes in which they did not perceive their immediate interests to be threatened.

A recent WFTU effort to encourage maritime and dock workers throughout the world to boycott Chilean ships is likely to have the same result, in spite of the militance of maritime workers and the near-universal condemnation of the Pinochet regime in trade union circles. If, however, increasing numbers of trade unionists fall under Communist influence, it will become much easier for the WFTU to promote political strikes—and, as American agribusiness and the Ford Administration discovered in 1975 when the dock workers refused to handle Soviet-bound grain, these strikes can be very disruptive in modern integrated economies.

There is also one issue-area, ostensibly nonpolitical, which the WFTU may be able to exploit in the future, namely, the multinational corporations. The WFTU has focused increasing attention on these companies. This in itself is not unusual. Both national and international non-Communist trade unions have felt increasingly threatened by these giant conglomerates, and have devoted a great deal of their energy to studying and trying to deal with them. The WFTU, however, has a somewhat different orientation. Unlike most non-Communist union organizations, it does not accept their existence, and does not believe that reform of national codes of conduct and the creation of countervailing trade union power are what is basically required to deal with the new multinational methods of production. Instead, Soviet-oriented trade unionists see these companies as simply another manifestation of capitalist society which must be destroyed. Reform will not save or really improve that society or its corporations. The WFTU believes in strong national control of the economy—basically

---

[73] See Godson, *op. cit.*

nationalization, with the national labor movement playing a major role in controlling the nationalized firms. But third, the Communists —and in this they are joined by non-Communists—believe workers should cooperate across state boundaries to protect their interests.

For the WFTU, however, cooperation across state boundaries means breaking down the barriers between Communist and non-Communist organizations, and then "coordinating" international labor activities to "defend" worker interests. The latter, of course, refers to more than an exchange of information and the multinational coordination of trade union bargaining strategy. It refers to manifestations of international solidarity, including the coordination of international strikes. Of course, the operations of Western multinationals in Eastern Europe and the Soviet Union are excluded from this category of actions. The WFTU has maintained that "action against the multinational companies is a question of class struggle in the capitalist countries."[74]

Just how the WFTU and its affiliates can coordinate international solidarity is uncertain. Certainly the WFTU is appealing to workers of all persuasions to break down the barriers set up by the "reactionary" forces and work together to deal with the new threat. When this appeal is restricted to cooperation between Communist and non-Communist unions dealing with the same company in different countries, or in international organizations such as the EEC, it is quite powerful. (How else can trade unions dealing with the Ford Motor Company or the Dunlop Tire Company gain sufficient unity and strength to influence the outcome of negotiations? Or how else can the workers in the European metal industry influence the EEC's regulations pertaining to multinationals unless they cooperate?) Whether the argument will be powerful enough however, remains to be seen.

Moreover, even if there is united action of some kind, coordinating and sustaining international strikes is no easy matter. Given the resources and dedication of the WFTU and Communist union leaders,

---

[74] For a comparison of the various international views on multinationals, see Everett M. Kassalow, "Attitudes towards the Multinationals," *Free Labor World,* June 1976, pp. 4–7. For a succinct statement by a WFTU official, see the interview with Pierre Baghi, *Flashes,* April 7, 1976.

It should also be pointed out that despite their public opposition to the multinationals, the Soviets and Eastern Europeans have dramatically increased their cooperation with these companies. See, for example, "Coping with Multinationals," *AFL-CIO Free Trade Union News,* December 1976.

however, international strikes may become a problem in the future. Certainly the WFTU is taking the subject seriously. Recently, the Secretariat took a number of steps to improve its ability to deal with multinationals. Secretary Akis Fantis was given responsibility for matters bearing on the subject, a standing working committee was established, and "a special WFTU body for trade union work in connection with these companies" also was created.[75]

Exactly how all the WFTU's activities are financed remains a mystery. Most probably the money comes from either the affiliates or directly from their governments. As over 70 percent of the affiliated membership comes from the Soviet Union and the Eastern bloc, it seems highly likely that the bulk of the funds originates in these countries, especially as the affiliates in Western Europe and the Third World for the most part are rather poor.[76] Whether the money comes in the form of dues or contributions from affiliated labor organizations, or whether is it derived from grants from governments is, of course, not very important. Clearly, the authorizing agents are the Soviet and European Communist Parties. Both the size and expenditure of the WFTU's regular administrative budget[77] and its international solidarity fund are determined ultimately by the national Party government officials.

The Soviets derive a number of advantages from their control of the WFTU, and it is a vehicle for promoting their objectives that would be difficult to replace. It is a channel for assisting legal and illegal Communist Parties and trade unions. It also provides them with access to a variety of non-Communist organizations that they would not enjoy on their own. It gives them a cloak of credibility that they would have difficulty obtaining independently, even though many people are aware that the Kremlin dominates the organization. It also helps them to weaken and reduce the appeal of the ICFTU and the ITS, the major international labor bodies in the non-Communist world.

---

[75] *Flashes,* March 17, 1976.

[76] A former WFTU official thinks the French CGT may have contributed to the WFTU, but he believes that except for token symbolic contributions the only other large Western affiliate, the Italian CGIL, has not.

[77] At the previously cited General Council meeting in 1975, the anticipated administrative budget for 1976, not counting the Solidarity Fund, was said to be $1.6 million.

But the WFTU also has its limitations. It is not always easy to control. The Soviets have had, and to some extent continue to have, difficulty in giving direction to some of their European affiliates and associates. Moreover, it is viewed by many in the non-Communist world as an anachronistic political organization that serves relatively little purpose, and it has on occasion been a hindrance to Soviet activities. For these reasons, the Soviets have developed their own bilateral relations with unions in the non-Communist world, particularly since the late 1960s. In this way, they are not forced to rely on the WFTU, and can appeal to unions which are reluctant to work with the organization. If the day comes when the WFTU appears to be a net liability, the Soviets will have other vehicles at their disposal.

Changing the Global Balance

Europe.   In recent years, the Soviets have not attempted to use European labor to bring a Communist Party to power, particularly in Central and Northern Europe. Rather, efforts have been made to use labor to support detente, weaken the region economically, and especially to increase the political influence of Moscow-oriented Communists. Further development of political influence might enable the Kremlin to use labor either to change the system of government in key West European countries, or to engage in sabotage and paramilitary activities in support of Soviet national security policy.

The promotion and exploitation of detente is one of the major activities of the Soviet international labor complex. The Soviets use labor as a propaganda vehicle to influence European voters and politicians. A major part of the peaceful coexistence effort in the trade union area is devoted to exchanges of thousands of delegations and the publication of multitudes of declarations. The Soviets and their allies spend a great deal of energy and very large sums on exchanges. For example, the Soviets report that whereas they exchanged several hundred delegations with 50 to 60 countries annually in the 1950s, they exchanged 1,500 delegations in 1974, over 1,700 in 1975, and they are now issuing joint declarations or "actively cooperating" with trade unions in 128 countries.[78] In West Germany particularly, the

---

[78] Morrell, *op. cit.,* pp. 562–567; "An AUCCTU Plenum," *Trud,* May 29, 1975; "U.S. Scored for Blocking USSR Trade Union Delegation Visas," *Tass,* July 13, 1976, FBIS. Pimenov claimed that during the past five years, the Soviets had received and sent abroad 9,500 delegations. See *Trud,* May 21, 1977.

pace of exchanges has risen dramatically. In 1970, for example, some 50 West German and East European union leaders traveled back and forth; in 1974, the figure was over 400. The British have followed suit. In 1975 alone, over 30 delegations from British unions visited the Soviet bloc, and the Soviets and East Europeans sent almost as many delegations to the UK.[79] Glowing accounts of these exchanges are printed in the Western commercial and labor press. (The East German news agency ADN, for example, quoted Jack Jones, the most important British union leader at the time, in 1976 as saying he had "felt at home" in the GDR.) In addition, the Soviets and the WFTU organize propaganda conferences and seminars almost monthly. These very widespread and costly activities have helped make detente respectable in trade union and Socialist circles, and have helped to reduce European labor's interest in an anti-Communist posture and in defense expenditures.

Second, the Soviets are trying to use organized labor to augment strains and tensions in Western society, or what is sometimes referred to as "the contradictions in capitalism." In Europe, this has meant promoting economic difficulties as well as strengthening unions and Communist Parties that can take advantage of the crisis of capitalism. As was discussed, the Soviets view the increasing economic crisis in the West, which had been expected to appear sooner or later, as a favorable trend. Moreover, while they did not engineer the Arab oil embargo and price rise, they have, within the limits of detente, encouraged the Arabs in these efforts.[80] At the same time, the increasing militance of the workers in England, France, Italy, and elsewhere —who have been hard hit by these developments—is seen as a natural defense of their interests in a capitalist economy, and is applauded and encouraged. The Kremlin, in other words, is helping to increase the strains in the West not only by encouraging the oil producers, but also by promoting trade union militance that in some cases is designed to hinder the "capitalist" economies still more.

Although the Kremlin today is not promoting the immediate use of strikes to bring down Western economies and systems of government, it is not unreasonable to conclude that it tries subtly to push

---

[79] *Economist Newspapers,* March 12, 1975, and July 7, 1976.
[80] See, for example, Robert O. Freedman, *Soviet Policy toward the Middle East* (New York: Praeger, 1975), p. 140.

in this direction whenever it promises a momentary payoff.[81] In Britain, the Soviets have helped in a small way to aggravate the country's economic difficulties by encouraging both Communist and non-Communist trade union leaders to take advantage of unsettled industrial relations and hyperinflation. For example, over the past ten years a major tactic employed by the British Communists, encouraged by the Soviets, was to join with non-Communists in trying to discredit the moderates, and to demand very high wage increases, frequently far above increases in the cost of living. If these very high wage claims succeeded, and some did, it further increased inflation and undermined confidence in the British economy; if they did not, the Communists blamed the moderate union officials and pushed for strikes, which also damaged the economy. In France, and most recently in Portugal, the Soviets have encouraged the Communist Parties and the unions they control to engage in similar tactics. In Italy, the Soviets and the Italian Communists for a while encouraged militant strike action "to defend the workers' interests." But now that the Italian Communist Party is seeking sufficient respectability to enter a coalition government, there has been much less emphasis on high wage claims and strikes. Indeed, the Communist Party and the CGIL have now become conservative in their demands.

The Soviets are also materially supporting trade union strike activities as well as organizations that they favor. It is impossible, of course, to ascertain the full extent of this support. Nevertheless, it is clear that they have assisted strike activities. On occasion, Communist-bloc financial support for a labor movement has been acknowledged.[82]

---

[81] Moscow also may not have pushed as hard as it could, as the Soviet leaders may have believed that this might endanger detente relations.

[82] Although it is impossible to determine the precise extent of Soviet financial support for European trade unions, the tip of what very well may be an iceberg can be seen. For example, according to Radio Moscow, August 11, 1972, Jimmy Reid, then Communist Secretary of the Scottish engineering workers, thanked the Soviet authorities for giving his union approximately $50,000 for strike actions. Cited in Brian Crozier, "Soviet Union's New Takeover Bid," *Forum World Features,* August 1973. In another Radio Moscow program, in January 1974, Leslie Dixon, a member of the Amalgamated Union of Engineering Workers Council, was quoted as saying that Soviet unions had made a substantial financial contribution to his union's "dispute fund." See Brian Crozier, "Soviet Interest in Industrial Unrest," *Soviet Analyst,* February 14, 1974. In another article, Crozier, Director of the Institute for the Study of Conflict, also lists several of the main KGB, AUCCTU, and CPUSSR Secretariat officials who he maintains are helping to coordinate strikes in Great Britain. "New Light on Soviet Subversion (1)," *ibid.,* March 28, 1974.

Although there is some statistical evidence to indicate that Communist Parties and Communist-controlled unions appear able to affect the prevalence of strike activity,[83] this should not be taken to mean that industrial strife and economic difficulties in Europe have been caused in the main by the Soviets. Almost certainly they have not. Rather, it would be closer to the truth to suggest that the Soviets have been encouraging European Communists to take advantage of whatever forces are at work to increase Western economic and political difficulties.

The third approach Moscow employs in the trade union area is the promotion of "working class unity" under its influence. For decades, the Kremlin has attached great importance to bringing Soviet labor organizations and Communist-controlled unions in the West into the mainstream of the international labor movement, primarily to give them much greater access to labor and political forces in the West. The Soviets expect Communists in the labor movement to become more influential as a result of this entree. Ultimately, they should be able to outmaneuver the non-Communists and gain complete control of almost the entire trade union movement.

Although they made a number of attempts to recover from the splits of the late 1940s and to recapture the unity that was achieved in the early postwar period, the Soviets did not meet with much success until the early 1970s.[84] Specifically, in addition to the bilateral

---

Former Secretary of State Kissinger estimated that in a 12-month period, the Soviet Union sent $50 million to the Portuguese Communist Party. *New York Times,* April 18, 1975. Undoubtedly, some of these funds were used to help establish Communist control of the Portuguese national trade union center, Intersindical. Indeed, Fletcher School of Law and Diplomacy professor and columnist John Roche has a photostat of a telegram from the Soviet Bank for Foreign Trade to a Lisbon bank transferring $28,570 to the Intersindical. "The Portuguese Labyrinth II," *King Features,* August 26, 1975. Moreover, in a rare acknowledgement of organization assistance, an East German labor leader stated that his organization has given the Portuguese unions one million escudos, and has promised additional aid for union buildings, duplicating machinery, and so forth. "Voice of the GDR," August 2, 1974 (BBC, SWB, EE/4669/A1/1).

[83] Douglas Hibbs, *Industrial Conflict in Advanced Industrial Societies* (Cambridge: Center for International Studies, Massachusetts Institute of Technology, April 1974).

[84] The best sources of information on trade union unification are polemical. The WFTU's monthly, *World Trade Union Movement,* carries at least one article on this subject almost every month. For a brief historical but critical analysis of Soviet policy, see Claude Harmel, *Est et Ouest,* March 1–15, 1975, pp. 12–24.

contacts they have now established with almost every European national center, they have successfully brought together the ICFTU's and WFTU's Euopean affiliates under the umbrella of the ILO, and they are encouraging more meetings of this kind. They also have encouraged, and have been the beneficiaries of, efforts to unify the European labor movement on a pan-European basis. The Communist-dominated Italian central body, CGIL, has been accepted into the recently formed European Confederation of Trade Unions (ETUC). The French Communist CGT has also applied for membership; and if it is admitted in the future, a move to bring in East European labor organizations can be expected.[85]

At the same time, the Soviets and the Communist labor organizations in Western Europe have encouraged unity in the industrial internationals. The French Communist CGT Printers Union (Fédération Française du Livre) succeeded in gaining entry into the International Graphic Workers Federation. Communist unions have also been admitted into one or two European trade secretariats, such as the European Metal Workers Federation. In Southern Europe, they have also made considerable headway. In Italy, the three main national centers—the Communist CGIL, the predominantly Catholic CISL, and the Socialist Unione Italiana del Lavoro (UIL), which broke away from the CGIL in the late 1940s—have created joint organizations for close collaboration, a compromise, instead of concluding earlier moves for organic unification.

In Portugal, the Communist Party, with Soviet support and assistance, has captured control of the Portuguese central labor body (Intersindical), but the democratic forces are fighting back. In Spain, Moscow-oriented Communists control many of the Workers Commissions, as well as many of the shop stewards of the official, government-controlled labor organization. But there, too, democratic trade unionists are fighting back, especially in the Basque and Catalan regions. The Soviets are also trying to secure closer cooperation with the revived Greek Confederation of Labor.

---

[85] On the origin and evolution of the ETUC, see John P. Windmuller, "European Regionalism: A new factor in international labor," *Industrial Relations Journal* (London), Summer 1976. On the relative success of the Soviets in Europe, see also Windmuller's "Realignment in the ICFTU: The Impact of Detente," *loc. cit.*

It should be noted that Moscow is pushing hard for the entry of European Communist-controlled unions into the mainstream of the European labor movement in spite of the Kremlin's strained relationship with some of the major Western Parties. Even in Italy, the most troublesome one of the Parties from the Soviet point of view, Moscow and the WFTU have lauded recent achievements at unification on the national level, as well as the CGIL's admission into the ETUC— and this in spite of the fact that to gain admission into the non-Communist body, the CGIL had to transform itself into an "associate" rather than an active member of the WFTU. Moscow seems to believe that it is more useful to strengthen the position of the European Communists in the non-Communist labor movement, even if it means weakening one of their own fronts. This also would seem to indicate that the strain between the Soviet and Italian Parties, at this stage anyway, has not led Moscow to stop supporting what it regards as important pro-Soviet forces on the continent.

In line with their doctrine, the Soviets and the European Communist Parties also are stressing the development of Communist strength in several sectors of the labor movement. They have placed considerable emphasis on building up Communist strength among workers in (a) new service, engineering, and technological industries (the new strata resulting from the "scientific and technical revolution")— what in France would be referred to as the "cadres"; (b) migratory workers, who can play a role in their host country in Northern Europe, as well as in Southern Europe and North Africa when they return home; and (c) the military. Perhaps based on the experience of Chile and Portugal, the Soviets now are seeking the support, or at least the neutrality, of what Timofeiev refers to as "progressive military personnel," which he says is a "prerequisite" for the world revolution.[86]

---

[86] The WFTU and TUIs have placed particular emphasis on the first two sectors. See, for example, the Charter of Demands adopted by the WFTU's International Trade Union Conference of Engineers, Managerial Staffs, and Technicians, in *World Trade Union Movement,* November 11, 1975; and the "Charter of Trade Union Rights and Economic and Social Demands of the Workers in Capitalist Countries" adopted by the Eighth WFTU Congress (Varna, 1973), in *Flashes,* May 26, 1976. The French, Italian, and small West German Communist Parties have also devoted considerable efforts to recruit and become influential in these sectors. It is more difficult to get information on the tactics that are used to penetrate the military.

Recent Soviet efforts to unify the Communist and non-Communist labor movements and gain control of various sectors, however, should not be taken to mean that the Soviets have been completely successful. Certainly they have not. While they have made considerable progress in this era of detente, Soviet and European Communists have not achieved full acceptance. The ICFTU as an institution still refuses to cooperate with the WFTU. The French CGT and the East Europeans have not been admitted into the ETUC. In Britain, leading Communist union leaders either have been defeated in union elections or have been forced to disavow their Party connection. Even in Italy, where the Communists are close to entry into government, organic unity between Communist and non-Communist central labor bodies has not been achieved. Thus, while the Soviets have good reason to be pleased with their efforts at working class unity thus far, they still have a way to go toward their ultimate goals.

The extent to which the Soviets have prepared or intend to use unions for paramilitary and espionage activities cannot be ascertained. Clearly, however, the Soviets are continuing to penetrate European unions. In West Germany, for example, the security services have arrested several Soviet-bloc agents in recent years who held senior union posts. Whether these individuals are assigned only to obtain information or also to become "agents of influence" in a major institution is unclear, but the Soviets obviously believe it is worth doing. There are also indications that they are developing sabotage capabilities through their connections in Western unions. Presumably Western security services have an accurate assessment of the bloc's capabilities and intentions, but only occasionally do tidbits of information on this subject come to light.[87]

It should be noted, however, that there may be a significant difference between the early postwar Soviet ability to manipulate European Communist Parties and trade unions and the current situation. Certainly the relationship has been complicated by a number of factors, such as detente, and the change of leadership and rapid turnover of Party membership in Europe. What was never an easy task was

---

[87] For a discussion of the KGB department which handles this subject, and the example of the British expulsion in 1971 of 105 "diplomats," several of whom were accused of working with British unions and preparing for sabotage activities, see John Barron, *KGB* (New York: Reader's Digest Press, 1974), especially pp. 320–330.

certainly made more difficult by such developments. Moreover, some students of European communism and labor also suggest that the Italian and French Parties no longer have complete control of the CGIL or CGT.[88]

Although the Soviets themselves maintain that they have not altered their goals or overall policy, a number of Western analysts maintain that there has been a fundamental policy shift, that detente is genuine. Others believe that the Soviet leaders, for a variety of domestic and international reasons, remain expansionist and are trying to weaken the West and increase their own power, although almost certainly they cannot manipulate even European Communist-oriented unions as effectively as they did immediately after World War II.

These interpretations and actual Soviet activities in the labor field are similar in some important respects to those that prevailed from 1945 to 1947. Then, too, there were two schools of thought about Soviet intentions, and Moscow's efforts to promote peaceful coexistence and unify the labor movement. After 1947, when the Kremlin adopted much tougher tactics and overtly used labor to impede European recovery and defense efforts, those Western political and trade union leaders who had been relatively sanguine about Soviet inten-

---

[88] Most observers believe that shortly after World War II, the major trade union centers in France and Italy fell under the control of Communist Parties subservient to Moscow. For discussion of the more complex current relationships between the Soviets and the major European Communist Parties, see Donald M. Blackmer and Annie Kriegel, *The International Role of the Communist Parties of Italy and France* (Cambridge: Center for International Studies, Harvard University, 1975); Donald M. Blackmer and Sydney Tarros, eds., *Communism in Italy and France* (Princeton: Princeton University Press, 1975); and Neil McInnes, *The Communist Parties of Western Europe* (London: Oxford University Press, 1975). Some writers differ on the extent of present Soviet and Communist Party control of the CGT and CGIL. See André Barjonet, *La CGT* (Paris: Seuil, 1968); the debate between Gerard Adam and Jean Ranger in *Revue Française de Science Politique,* June 1968, pp. 524–539, and December 1968, pp. 182–187; and Jean-Daniel Reynaud, "Trade Unions and Political Parties in France: Some Recent Trends," *Industrial Relations Review,* January 1975, pp. 208–226. Walter Kendall in *The Labor Movement in Europe* (London: Allen Lane, 1975) argues that the CGT and CGIL are still controlled by the French and Italian Communist Parties; and the French journals *Les Études Sociales et Syndicales* and *Est et Ouest* provide detailed information to indicate that the CGT and CGIL are still controlled by Communist Parties that remain basically loyal to Moscow. For an example of a commentator who believes that the CGIL is no longer an instrument of the Italian Communist party, see Peter R. Weitz, "Labor and Politics in a Divided Movement," *Industrial and Labor Relations Review,* January 1975, pp. 226–243.

tions and capabilities changed their position. Today, a number of pessimists on both sides of the Atlantic, while recognizing that a more complex relationship exists now between the Soviets and the European labor movement, are again sounding the alarm.

United States. The Soviets have also tried to influence American labor, but up until the present, at any rate, they have been spectacularly unsuccessful. Nevertheless, they are stepping up their efforts, in the belief that the crisis of capitalism and the coming generational change in the AFL-CIO will offer new opportunities. They are also seeking to take advantage of the breakup of the anti-Communist liberal-labor coalition in the United States. For example, they are trying to promote detente by encouraging Soviet and American trade union leader exchanges. In spite of the fact that these types of exchanges have been achieved in almost every other profession, and some senior US government officials have also encouraged them, so far there have been almost no labor exchanges. Indeed, even Soviet efforts to send "trade union" delegations to the United States generally have failed so far.

Until now, this has been due to a policy decision by the Department of State not to recommend waivers of visa ineligibility (members of Communist organizations must secure a waiver to enter the United States) in the case of Soviet bloc labor officials wishing to visit on trade union matters. (Bloc labor officials can and sometimes do visit the United States on tourist or other kinds of visas.) This policy has been based on foreign policy considerations as well as the attitude of the AFL-CIO on this question.[89] This policy has confounded the

---

[89] The policy and rationale were restated in a letter from Assistant Secretary for Congressional Relations Robert J.McCloskey to Congressman Donald M. Fraser on July 6, 1976, who sought clarification of US policy. The letter also indicated that the policy did not violate the agreement on the free exchange of persons embodied in CSCE (Helsinki) Final Act of 1974. McCloskey wrote that "the provision for contacts and exchanges in the labor field was raised and discussed during the CSCE negotiations. In signing the agreement, all the participants were then aware of our longstanding policy and they accepted our position against inclusion of any reference to such exchanges. . . . We do not consider that the denial of visas to the Soviet labor representatives in any way diminishes our efforts to encourage the Soviet Union to improve its performance in the area of human rights embodied in the 'Basket Three' provisions of the Final Act." This position has been restated by the Carter Administration. See the Secretary of State's *Second Annual Report to the Commission on Security and Cooperation in Europe, December 1, 1976–June 1, 1977,* Special Report No. 34, June 1977, p. 21.

Soviets. They find it particularly galling when they want to demonstrate that the American people, and particularly the working class, is in favor of detente, and that the AFL-CIO leadership is unrepresentative of American labor. As the *Trud* correspondent in the United States put it: "It is hard to explain this phenomenon and to understand why the State Department carries out so obediently the whims of a labor union leader living in the past."[90]

Indeed, in spite of criticism from liberal academics, the liberal press, some State Department officials, and some unions, and the Soviet promise of increasing jobs from Soviet-American trade, the AFL-CIO has refused to abandon its long-time opposition to exchanges with government-controlled labor organizations—whether of the left or the right. Moreover, not only have the Soviets been unable to use most American unions to promote detente, as they have been able to do in most national centers in Europe, but they have been faced with trade unions which have been among the major critics of the Soviet concept of detente. The 1976 AFL-CIO invitation to A. Solzhenitsyn was one of a number of examples of the AFL-CIO's efforts to stop what it regarded as the Nixon and Ford Administration's major foreign policy blunder.[91]

Whether the mainstream of American labor will continue its traditional opposition to exchanges with labor organizations in the Soviet bloc, and devote attention and resources to promoting the cause of Soviet dissidents in the future, and whether the US government will continue to refuse visas to Soviet labor officials, is uncertain. There are strong pressures for change. In the short run, policymakers in the Executive Branch have decided to take advantage of a recent amendment to the law applying to visa ineligibility to admit Communist labor officials. As a result, those American union leaders interested in meeting with them may be able to encourage other union leaders to participate in their gatherings. On the other hand, the AFL-CIO Executive Council is highly unlikely in the near future to reverse its longstanding position on meeting with Soviet bloc officials.[92]

Soviet efforts to use labor to influence or weaken the American economy also have been unsuccessful. Ever since the late 1940s,

---

[90] *Trud,* December 29, 1975.
[91] See this writer's "American Labor's Continuing Involvement in World Affairs," *Orbis,* Spring 1975, for further details.
[92] *Ibid.*

when the CIO purged the Communists from its ranks, the Moscow-controlled Communist Party has been trying to build up Communist cells in several major industries, such as steel and auto manufacturing. With rare exceptions, they have made very little headway. Nevertheless they continue these efforts, sometimes openly and sometimes secretly.[93]

Although the Soviets and their local Communist allies cannot hope to unify the American labor movement under their control, they are seeking to gain greater influence within the labor movement and to weaken the impact of the AFL-CIO on the international scene. American Communist union officials have not been agreed on just how to do this. One school of thought, including senior Communist Party functionaries such as Gus Hall and George Morris, seems to have believed it was hopeless to try to gain great influence in the AFL-CIO. Ironically, although they were for "world labor unity," they proposed instead splitting the AFL-CIO and creating a new central body of the more "progressive" AFL-CIO unions like the Steelworkers, Meat Cutters, and AFSCME, and unaffiliated unions like the UAW and the United Mine Workers. In this new structure, the more "conservative," anti-Communist union leadership would be weakened and the Communists would have a greater chance to maneuver. A second school, consisting for the most part of old-time Communist CIO officials still active in unions like the United Electrical Workers, Local 1199 of the Hospital Workers, and District 65 of the Distributive Workers, wanted to build up their strength in the AFL-CIO. They reasoned that when George Meany departs the scene, they will be in a better position to influence the mainstream of the labor movement if they remain a part of it.

Whatever the tactics, the Soviets and their Communist Party allies are working hard to gain influence in a number of unions. Apart from the AUCCTU, Communist Party, and KGB staff working on the United States in the Soviet Union, a "labor specialist" has been openly

---

[93] For a discussion of Communist tactics and success, particularly on the waterfront in the 1930s and 1940s, see Robert Morris, *No Wonder We Are Losing* (Plano, Texas: University of Plano Press, 1958). Morris was a senior counterintelligence officer in the New York naval district in the 1940s. See also Philip Selznik, *The Organizational Weapon* (New York: McGraw Hill, 1952). For more recent activities, see "Communist Party USA Attempts to Penetrate the Trade Union Movement," *Hearings,* Committee on Internal Security, House of Representatives, 93rd Congress, 1st Session, November 28, 1973.

assigned to the Soviet Embassy in Washington for the first time. In the Fall of 1975, Ruben A. Grigorian arrived in Washington with the title of First Secretary. Previously, he had been a Secretary of the Metalworkers TUI and member of the AUCCTU staff. He and the *Trud* correspondent in Washington work with the WFTU's official representative to the United Nations, the former UE official Ernest de Maio, to analyze trends and opportunities.[94] Sometimes they are joined in these deliberations by the key Soviet official in the WFTU Secretariat, Boris Averyanov. Averyanov, who in his former capacity as Director of the AUCCTU International Affairs Department had difficulty entering the United States because of the State Department's visa policy, can travel practically at will to the United Nations in New York.

Apart from trying to arrange for labor exchanges and gaining support for Soviet foreign policy positions, these men also are in touch with loyal CPUSA officials working in the labor area. The CPUSA, apart from recruiting a small number of youngsters, training them, and assigning them to trade union work, also participated in setting up a number of front organizations which deal with economic and political trade union issues not necessarily identified with the Communist Party—for example, the National Coordinating Committee for Trade Union Action and Democracy (TUAD). The major purpose of this committee is ostensibly to promote more effective unions and a greater degree of democracy within unions. In fact, however, the committee is part of the Soviet bloc's effort to remove unsympathetic union leaders and gain greater influence by supporting a challenger.

The bloc's major concerns are, of course, union leaders who support AFL-CIO foreign policy. Views on domestic legislation or collective bargaining are not the major criteria in the Soviet and CPUSA's decision to support a given leader. Nor does the union official's loyalty to the Soviet cause always appear to be a decisive factor. Indeed, by supporting individuals who are not Communists

---

[94] Other diplomats and journalists also may play an important role in these deliberations. A. Mkrtchian, for example, formerly a member of the CPSU Central Committee's International Department, is the author of a recent book on trends in the American labor movement. Until recently, Mkrtchian was also a senior Soviet official in Washington. Similarly, a *Tass* correspondent in New York, Nicolay Setunskiy, published a book in 1977 entitled, *USA Trade Unions and Politics*.

and whom they do not control, but who are opposed to the current AFL-CIO posture, Moscow appears to be demonstrating increasing sophistication in trying to weaken "the main enemy."

The CPUSA, for example, will either join a rank-and-file challenge to a selected leader, or will set up a "rank-and-file movement" on its own. Apparently, there are four or five "rank-and-file movements" under way at the present time, and sometimes it becomes difficult to distinguish the non-Communist rank-and-file challenge from Soviet-financed and -supported efforts. However, although TUAD was part of Edward Sadlowski's unsuccessful challenge in the February 1977 elections in the Steelworkers, so far the Communists have not done very well. Indeed, as the older generation of able US Communist union leaders passes from the scene (such as James Matles and Harry Bridges), very few younger American Communists have stepped into their shoes. On the other hand, as the older generation of anti-Communist American labor leaders passes from the scene, the small number of active Communists, though perhaps less able, may find it easier to maneuver and coalesce with the younger generation of trade union leaders who may not be as sensitive to the problems of working with Communists.

In addition, the splintering of the Democratic Party's long-time coalition of liberals and labor also presents the Soviets with new opportunities. For most of the postwar period, labor and liberal intellectuals and politicians worked together on a number of economic and national security issues. From the perspective of labor, however, the liberals now tend to be too conservative on economic issues and too weak or "soft" on foreign policy. To retain liberal support for labor's position on domestic issues, some union leaders—and particularly the younger generation—may be willing to jettison a position that for many of them is of secondary importance for the labor movement, namely, a "hard line" on foreign policy. In this situation, the Soviets and their local allies should find it easier to build relationships with some sections of the American labor movement.

Third World.   Unlike Western Europe, the Soviets do not have much of a trade union base in the non-Western world. But they do try to take advantage of any opportunities available to them. Sometimes they are interested in short-term high payoffs, and will try to increase their influence quickly and directly. They will, for example, take advantage of their assets, and encourage or allow their trade union clients to bring a friendly regime to power, as they tried to do in Ecuador in 1971.[95] At other times, they are willing to sacrifice short-term gains for long-term influence. For example, on occasion they have ordered the local Communist Party to dissolve its small trade union apparatus and merge with the main central labor body (for example, in Syria and Iraq) in the hope that, in the future, the Communists will be more influential, or because they do not want to offend the government in question.

There are several prongs in Soviet labor strategy. First, a major part of their effort in the non-Western world is devoted to exploiting the considerable anti-Western sentiment in the less developed countries. Whether it is "reactionary feudalism," "neoimperialism," and Israeli "repression" in the Middle East, poverty and apartheid in Africa, or the rise of military dictatorship in Latin America, the Soviets maintain that the cause of the problem is the Western powers, and particularly the United States. This enables them to increase their own influence and sometimes the influence of their local allies, and correspondingly reduce the influence of local Western-oriented political and trade union elements that do not accept these explanations. It also provides them with the basis for coalescing with non-Western officials at international governmental and nongovernmental forums, and lays the groundwork for "labor unity."

Second, as already pointed out, the Soviet bloc has also encouraged Third World trade unionists to weaken the West by more direct means. Third World labor movements are encouraged to protest and sometimes impede efforts of the United States in particular to gain base rights or secure the cooperation of non-Western governments. The Soviets and the WFTU also exhort them to follow the example of the Persian Gulf rulers, and to renegotiate trading arrangements and demand much higher terms from the West—which will, of course, increase inflation and affect the Western economies adversely. Third, the Soviets lay great stress on "labor unity" under their influence on the national, regional, and global levels. In this essentially political approach to unify labor under their control, the Soviets demonstrate great flexibity in their tactics.

Ideally, they strive to dominate the major trade union centers in a given country. This is not expected to happen overnight, or without

---

[95] James D. Theberge, *The Soviet Presence in Latin America* (New York: Crane, Russak, 1974), pp. 35–36.

great expenditures of energy and resources. If possible, they first establish bilateral relations with national trade union centers. Initial contact will be made either by the AUCCTU itself or, if this is not possible or desirable, by a Soviet or East European embassy official. The Soviets will suggest an exchange of delegations, friendly visits, or study trips. If these are successful, there will be an escalation of the relationship—joint seminars, conferences, standing committees, permanent committees, and other, permanent organizational links. Sometimes, they will seek to influence or corrupt individual labor leaders by offering them free trips, cars, money, equipment, and the like. The Soviets will also arrange for advisors to be stationed in a non-Western country; for example, the East German Gunter Goldburg was stationed in Zambia, and a Syrian Communist was sent to advise the Kuwaiti unions in the 1960s. Scholarships either at the AUCCTU or East European labor schools, or sometimes at Patrice Lumumba University or the French CGT school, will be provided for local union officials. Friendly local leaders or their organizations will be offered crucial financial subsidies, and sometimes extremely close and cooperative relationships will be developed between the non-Western unions and the Soviet labor complex. But these very close relationships usually develop only where the governments of the day enjoy a good relationship with the Soviet Union, as the Ghanaian government did in the early 1960s, or the Nigerian government in the early 1970s.[96] Sometimes the Soviets will even insist that Communists dissolve their own party and trade union apparatus and enter into the only legal central labor body, which the Soviets are supporting, whether the local Communist Parties agree or not.

There are, however, many cases where the local government will refuse the Soviets direct access because it is suspicious of Soviet intentions or wishes to preserve its nonaligned image. In these situations, the Soviets will either work through the WFTU or regional bodies such as ICATU and OATUU, which try to sustain a balancing

---

[96] A major section of the Nigerian trade unions has been supported by the Soviet Union for a number of years. For an unusually detailed account of this operation in the late 1960s (including the names of Soviet officials, the huge sums involved, and how they passed the funds), see the articles of the University of Masachusetts political scientist Dr. Arnold Beichman in the *International Herald Tribune*, January 24–25, 1970. Reference has already been made to the documents revealing the relationship between the Ghanaians and the Soviet labor complex.

act between pro-Soviet and pro-Western organizations. In the Persian Gulf, for example, the conservative rulers will not allow the Soviets legally to train officials for the incipient labor movement in places such as Bahrein. But as part of a WFTU-ICATU seminar, Bahreini and other migratory workers from the region, who may end up in Bahrein or other countries in the area, can attend. And sometimes, if even this degree of identification with the Soviet bloc would prevent individuals from attending, training is undertaken by "friendly" trade union centers (for example, in Syria, Iraq, or South Yemen) without overt identification with the Soviet bloc.[97]

One of the best illustrations of Soviet orchestration of its international labor complex to gain influence in the Third World can be found in its support of the PLO labor organization. In an interview in 1975, a senior PLO official with responsibility for labor told this writer that over the previous six years, approximately 20 groups of three to four Palestinians had been trained in East European labor schools. This included virtually all PLO officials concerned with labor, and the interviewee himself had been trained in Eastern Europe, as well as at ICATU schools in Cairo and Damascus. In addition, the PLO labor organization (then located in southern Lebanon, Syria, and Egypt, with small branches in Western Europe to deal with Palestinian guest workers) received a subsidy every three years from the WFTU and ICATU, as well as the PLO. (The PLO itself received money and support from a number of Communist and Arab governments.) In addition, the PLO labor organization also received food, clothing, and medicines which originated in the Soviet Union and Eastern Europe. But the official claimed that few of the top PLO labor officials were Communists. Of the top seven, six had no party identification; and one, he admitted, was a Syrian Baathist. Below the top level, however, a number of the officials were either Baathist or had become Communists.

It is difficult to determine with any real accuracy how much influence the Soviet international labor complex can wield in the short and long run. Certainly this will vary from place to place and accord-

---

[97] *Baghdad Observer,* for example, reported on May 6, 1975, that the 12th Arab two-week course held in Iraq had just graduated 40 Palestinian workers from the Gulf, Egypt, Lebanon, and Libya. (The Iraqis, Syrians, and South Yemenis, for that matter, probably utilize these training sessions to increase their own influence in the region at the same time.)

ing to circumstances. On the one hand, it is easy to conclude, as many have done, that organized labor does not play a significant role in the politics of non-Western countries. The wage-earning forces in most of these countries account for only a small percentage of the population (frequently no more than ten to 15 percent), and the number of unionized workers is even smaller. The difficulties of organization are accentuated by ethnic, racial, religious, and linguistic differences, especially in Africa and many parts of Asia. Moreover, the Third World is frequently characterized by an abundant supply of unskilled labor, a high proportion of skilled migrant labor (for example, in the Persian Gulf), employer hostility, and a low level of political consciousness.

In many countries, however, organized labor has great political potential, and sometimes does play an important role. During the colonial period, the unions, sometimes directly linked with the nationalist parties and sometimes in a set of loose, short-term alliances with other groups, played a significant role in preindependence politics as well as in the independence struggle, for example, in Africa north and south of the Sahara.[98] Second, labor is one of the few organized sectors in a Third World country. In most of these societies, political institutions are weak, party structures usually either feeble or completely nonexistent, bureaucracies deficient, communications poor, and there are few interest groups other than the Army and perhaps the students associations. In this situation, the trade unions represent—for all their deficiencies—a relatively co-ordinated and articulate pressure group. They have the capacity to make demands at the expense of other, less organized and less articulate sectors of society.

Of course, the army has the best chance to intervene politically, and the capacity to impose permanent control. But as numerous cases in the non-Western world illustrate (Goulart's Brazil in 1964, Allende's Chile in the early 1970s, the Popular Republic of the Congo after 1963, the Sudan since 1958, Ethiopia in 1973, and Dahomey—almost permanently since 1951) political intervention by the army and the trade unions is not mutually exclusive. As Robin

---

[98] See, for example, the discussion of North Africa in Willard Beiling, *Modernization and African Labor, A Tunisian Case Study* (New York: Praeger, 1965); and the analysis of central and southern Africa in Robin Cohen, *Labor and Politics in Nigeria, 1945–1971* (London: Heineman, 1974), pp. 240–245.

Cohen has pointed out, a large-scale strike in Africa often has a wider significance than the special claims of wage earners. If a confrontation is sufficiently sharp and sustained, and if it is relayed by ambitious groups, perhaps with a wider social vision, it can evolve into a fundamental challenge to a regime.[99]

Moreover, unions occupy a strategic position in the economy and administration of a country. They are based in the key urban centers. (If the number of unionists relative to the number of urbanized inhabitants of a country is measured, rather than comparing their number to the total population, the numerical importance of the trade unions becomes more significant.) The government and public corporations also are invariably the most important employers in numerical terms (in many African countries, the government employs about half the wage-earning population), so that any major industrial action has at least implicit political consequences. When these actions take place in strategic public sectors, such as the railways, docks, and post and telegraph, the unions have even greater political leverage.[100]

The unions, despite their small numerical strength, also have considerable propaganda strength and can influence the opinions of a sizeable number of their own members, as well as people outside the union structure. This influence derives from the relatively elevated status of the wage earners and their location in the process of political socialization and communication. (Workers may migrate to the city, where they are socialized; and when they return to the countryside, even if only for brief periods of time, they are listened to by their relatives and friends in the rural areas.)[101] Finally, the living circumstances of the worker frequently dispose him to hold distinct social attitudes and to take collective action. He has been wrenched away from many of the traditional social controls, and often is the victim of overcrowded cities with poor housing and sanitation, incompetent police forces, and sometimes even a breakdown in the network of food distribution. In these circumstances, labor movements can become the focus of enormous discontent.

These and other factors explain the opportunities and the predisposition of the unions to play an important political role. In spite of

---

[99] Cohen, *op. cit.*, pp. 245–252.
[100] *Ibid.*
[101] See, for example, *ibid., passim;* and John H. Magill, *Labor Unions and Political Socialization, A Case Study of Bolivian Workers* (New York: Praeger, 1974).

the fact that after independence, political parties are able to effect a measure of control over most interest groups, the ease with which they are overthrown, usually by the military, indicates that the political process in the first years after independence is complex. Parties are rarely strong in and of themselves, and decisions are made as a result of bargaining with major groups both inside and outside the party. Sometimes the ruling party has been able to subordinate the unions under its control (for example, Nyerere's Tanzania, Nkrumah's Ghana, and Sekou Toure's Guinea); at other times, there was a partnership (Kenyatta's Kenya, Bourguiba's Tunisia, Houphouet-Boigny's Ivory Coast); and at other times, the unions were aligned with important opposition parties (Morocco, Botswana, and Albert Margai's Sierra Leone in the 1960s).

Even under military rule, unions can have considerable political leverage. The army on its road to political power, or once it has assumed power, may attempt to include in its base a wider section of the population; and the unions, which are not part of the old order, provide a useful base of legitimacy. (A good example of this strategy would be Major N'Gouabi's Congo-Brazzaville since 1969). In other instances, after a coup the Army factionalizes, and the factions bid for the support of various institutions, as in the case of the "insecure" army in the Sudan since 1958.[102] In Latin America, military rulers sometimes have felt it necessary to seek the cooperation of one part of the labor movement in order to contain what they regard as a more dangerous threat to their rule from another part. For example, in Peru (1969-71) and Honduras (1975-76), the military allied with the Communist-led unions against the non-Communitsts.

Yet another pattern emerges in the case of Dahomey-Benin. There the country is divided into roughly three regional power blocs, and it is essential for the power contestants, whether military or civilian, to control the capital of Cotonou. Through the early 1970s, no political faction of note was able to control Cotonou without the support of the unions.[103]

No doubt other patterns and relationships between labor and the governments of the Third World will emerge in the future; but under these circumstances, Soviet influence in the labor movement of Third World countries becomes significant. Although the Soviets began to

---

[102] Cohen, *op. cit.*, pp. 252–260.
[103] *Ibid.*

train cadres for work in these areas even during the days of the colonial regimes, they did not mount a major effort until the late 1950s. As was discussed above, they do not expect their efforts over the last 20 years to result in a monopoloy of power for Moscow-oriented political groups. But they have already reaped some benefits, and continue to look at the Third World as a long-range goal.

Africa. In Africa, the Soviets have had some success which has yielded political benefits. But they have also suffered setbacks. Until recently, at least, Moscow has concentrated on trying to build up politically reliable cadres in the top echelons of the unions, rather than attempting to build mass organizations which could serve the bread-and-butter interests of the workers.

In North Africa, they have had little success. The Communist Parties remain small and, for the most part, underground organizations. Even where the Soviets have run training programs and exchanged delegations and communiques, the impact has been minor. The best example of this is Morocco, where in spite of a fairly cooperative relationship with the head of the Union Marocain du Travail (UMT), which is the center of opposition to the King, very few Moroccan union leaders have become Communists. Nor are they enamored with the Soviet regime, although by and large they have had little contact with, and are not particularly well disposed toward, the West.[104] In Tunisia, the Soviets have had even less success. The Tunisian unions remain affiliated to the ICFTU and maintain friendly relations with the AFL-CIO. It is quite possible, however, that in Algeria and Libya, where the governments are more friendly with the Soviet Union and the unions usually follow the government line, the Soviets may have made more headway.

In sub-Saharan Africa, there is a similar pattern. In some countries, such as Somalia and Congo-Brazzaville, whose governments have been very friendly to the Soviet Union, the "unions" also follow this line. Their top leadership is trained by the Soviets, the national centers are affiliated to the WFTU, and they cooperate with the Soviets in international forums. The strength of this loyalty among the union leadership is not easy to determine. As the case of post-Nkrumah Ghana reveals, once pressure from the government ceases, an anti-Soviet leadership can come to the fore quite easily.

In other countries, the Soviets for years have been training leaders

---

[104] Interviews with UMT officials, June 1976.

and spending large sums to support friendly labor leaders (for example, in Nigeria), but so far they have had little to show for it. Sometimes, as in the Sudan, where a large Communist Party and trade union movement loyal to Moscow had been built up, the Communist leadership was literally wiped out by the new military regime and Moscow has had to start again. In other countries, such as the Ivory Coast, Senegal, and Zaire, the Soviets have been virtually frozen out.

On the other hand, sometimes Soviet training and support has paid off. Even when it may appear that they have made almost no progress, they have managed to secure an influential base as a result of their training programs and their subsidies. An interesting case in point is Ethiopia. In the Spring of 1974, the relatively free and Western-oriented Confederation of Ethiopian Trade Unions (CELU) succeeded in organizing a general strike, which together with student disruptions was a major factor in leading the army to overthrow Emperor Haile Selassie. After the CELU leadership claimed the military were practically as oppressive as the Emperor's regime, the organization was closed down, only to be reborn a few months later. The new leaders had no previous CELU background. Instead, they had been selected by the Soviet Embassy for training in Moscow. After taking over CELU, they adopted Moscow's political line; and in a June 1975 statement, claimed that CELU previously had been supporting imperialism and the policies of the ICFTU and the AFL-CIO, instead of the progressive line of the WFTU. As a result, it was necessary to sever all relations with the AFL-CIO and establish relations with "all progressive organizations of the broad masses."

This, of course, is not to say that the unions in Ethiopia will remain in the hands of pro-Soviet elements. Just as they and the military took advantage of the chaos surrounding the demise of Haile Selassie to take over the unions, they could be overthrown in another outbreak of unrest. But this does illustrate that in its long-term approach, Moscow has on occasion been able to take advantage of opportunities to place agents of influence in control of important institutions.

In Southern Africa, the Soviets' long term strategy has already paid off in the former Portuguese colonies, and the Soviets have been preparing for an influential role in postapartheid South Africa. In

Angola and Mozambique, they had for years been supporting and training the MPLA and FRELIMO military and trade union leaders who eventually emerged as the victorious elements. As a result, the new leaders of the labor movement in these areas were basically pro-Soviet, and Moscow and the WFTU have continued to provide them with subsidies, training, and the like.[105]

In South Africa, the Soviets cannot operate legally; and the underground organizations they support, the South African Communist Party, the African National Congress, and the South African Confederation of Trade Unions (SACTU), currently have little influence. In a postapartheid South Africa, however, the Soviets—as a result of their training and support of South African refugees and underground organizations—will have trained leaders who can step into the breach. As they did recently in Portugal, Spain, and Ethiopia, pro-Soviet forces may well emerge from obscurity to control strategic sectors of the society—unless, of course, there is alternative leadership unmarked by their association with the current regime. In Botswana, Lesotho, and Swaziland, however, the Soviets appear to have little influence, either through contacts, training, or by gaining an influential base in the leadership of the labor movement.

Middle East. Moscow's influence in the labor movement in the Middle East varies from country to country. In countries where the regime is friendly to the Soviet Union, there is a close cooperative relationship between the Soviet international labor complex and local labor organizations. This is true especially in Iraq, South Yemen, and —until the Summer of 1976 anyway—in Syria. As was discussed above, the Soviets cooperate on propaganda and training both in these countries, and through them, in the region as a whole. As the Arab states, and particularly the Persian Gulf, industrialize, this may be very important indeed, especially as there is almost no countervailing anti-Soviet trade union presence in the area.

The extent of Soviet influence in Egypt, however, where the unions until Nasser's time had a tradition of independence, is not as extensive as might be thought. In spite of close association with and training by the bloc for the past 20 years, pro-Soviet forces have not become

---

[105] See, for example, *Flashes,* February 25, 1976, and September 10, 1976, for a joint UNTA and WFTU communique.

dominant either in the Egyptian Federation of Labor (EFL) or in the Egyptian-run ICATU. This is not for want of trying. In both the EFL and ICATU, the Soviets tried to help friendly Arabs become dominant. Under the encouragement of the Sadat regime, however, non-Communist leaders have resisted; and in ICATU, the Egyptians were able to mobilize support from the Moroccan, Tunisian, and Lebanese labor movements to resist Soviet, Syrian, and Libyan efforts to take over in the early 1970s. But the struggle inside both the EFL and ICATU is not over. There is a great deal of Nasserite and pro-Soviet sentiment in the trade unions, as well as in some intellectual and political circles, which worries the Sadat government.[106]

Asia. In Southern and Southeast Asia, the Soviets not only have to contend with governments that are wary of their influence, but also with Peking-oriented Communists. With the exception of India and one or two small beachheads in the Pacific, such as Fiji and East Timor, however, the Soviets have little influence in trade union circles in the area. But they are stepping up their efforts in the area. They are concentrating on exchanges of delegations and the training of a small number of friendly Asians both in the Soviet Union and Eastern Europe, and locally through the WFTU and its Indian affiliate, AITUC. As already mentioned, however, very few Asian labor organizations so far have been willing to affiliate with the WFTU, and the Soviets have not been able to work through a regional labor body. Nevertheless, the WFTU is organizing regional education conferences, establishing a "permanent representation" in the area, and promoting "various measures and activities aimed at holding a United Trade Union Conference." The WFTU has also organized seminars in Australia; and according to the Prime Minister of New Zealand: "There is a constant stream of militant members of the New Zealand trade unions going to Moscow and other East European capitals for indoctrination and training, and this year that activity has been stepped up considerably."[107] If, in addition, the major split in the international Communist movement healed, Soviet and Chinese cooperation in local movements would give the Soviets much more potential influence in the area.[108]

---

[106] Interviews with EFL leaders, June 1976.
[107] R. D. Muldoon, "Address to the Navy League of New Zealand," November 25, 1976.
[108] On Soviet activities in Asia, see G. N. Mikaya, "The Soviet Trade Unions'

Latin America and the Caribbean.   In Central and South America and the Caribbean, the Soviets and the Cubans have also stepped up their efforts, taking advantage of certain recent political trends. One is the industrial revolution, which is taking place in many parts of the region. The ensuing instability and turmoil, both in urban and rural areas, creates unfulfilled expectations as well as misery and discontent, which have often been fertile grounds for Communist agitation. The growth of nationalism and anti-Americanism is another factor which facilitates Communist penetration. In this atmosphere, it is relatively easy for the Soviets and their local allies to identify with the anti-American imperialist front. A third factor which may help pro-Soviet elements is the rise of right-wing dictatorships in the region. Maintaining power by eliminating those institutions that stand in their way, and frequently by brutal suppression, these authoritarian governments may be helping the Soviet-backed minority to rally all those opposed to the regime, propose farreaching "democratic" reforms, ally themselves with other parties and trade unionists, even those that are anti-Communist, and eventually assume control of the anti-regime coalition. Flaunting their socalled antidictatorial reputation as well as the organizations they have created, the Communists then have posed as the champions of democracy. As a result of employing this strategy, Moscow-oriented Communists have done extremely well in Spain and Portugal, and now are seeking similar successes in Chile and Uruguay, for example.

Capitalizing on these trends, the Soviets have begun to bring their whole international apparatus to bear on the region. They have also been able to take advantage of Cuba's claimed status as a nonaligned, Third World nation, and the Cuban Communist Party and trade unions are playing a major role in Soviet efforts.

Because Latin America is viewed as a more advanced area, with an urban and to some extent rural proletariat, unlike Africa and Asia, the Soviets have concentrated on building up Communist Parties and trade union organizations, both in urban and rural areas. In many countries, there is a daily Party or trade union newspaper. The Communist union officials can also call on the services of Communist labor lawyers; and in a number of countries, the Communists offer a

Solidarity with the Struggle of the Asian Countries' Trade Unions," *Narody Azii, I Afriki,* October 13, 1975; and "A WFTU Program for Asia," *World Trade Union Movement,* January 1977, p. 14.

variety of medical, welfare, and trade union services to workers.[109] The WFTU, CPUSTAL, and local Communist unions also have been organizing an increasing number of training seminars, as well as financing training in Cuba and the Soviet bloc.

So far, however, Moscow has not been able to wield great influence in the labor movement in the region. Communist-controlled unions are for the most part small and weak. Until recently, most of them were affiliated with CPUSTAL, which (as already discussed) was also very weak. Some 14 of these small centers (including Martinique and Guadeloupe) now have affiliated openly with the WFTU.

The Soviets, and particularly the Cubans, have increased their over-all labor activities in the past few years. In several places, for example in Honduras, Soviet- and Cuban-supported Communists have succeeded in gaining control of important unions. In Jamaica, Guyana, and other places, they also are becoming increasingly influential. Whether Moscow will be able to continue to capitalize on trends in this and other parts of the world will depend on a number of factors, including the conclusions drawn by policymakers in the democratic world, and particularly in the United States.

---

[109] Reliable, detailed information on Communist labor activities is difficult to come by. One of the few attempts to gather information can be found in *Anti-Democratic Labor Activities in Latin America, Report of an Informal Survey,* Georgetown University International Labor Program, Washington, D. C., Summer 1976.

Conclusion

Although some may argue that the Kremlin has lost interest in the use of organized labor as an instrument of policy, this would not appear to be the case. While the Soviets have acquired superpower status and may place greater emphasis on state-to-state relations and traditional instruments of statecraft such as military and economic aid than ever before, they are still employing a transnational strategy, attempting to influence both governments and important nongovernmental sectors throughout the world. There seems little doubt that for them the labor instrument, like the military instrument, is one of a number of means of affecting political conditions in the non-Communist world. Soviet leaders and analysts stress the importance of the subject; and past Soviet practice indicates that for some time, labor has been seen and used as a political tool. Today, the Kremlin continues to devote considerable attention, resources, and manpower to weakening Western influence and gaining control of the labor sector abroad.

The full significance of the labor instrument, however, is not always immediately apparent. Viewed in isolation, organized labor in the non-Communist world, even under Soviet influence, would not necessarily appear to be important. The labor movement, however, as has been shown, can affect public policy, the power of a government to rule, and even the continued existence of a political system. Interacting with political parties, the military, and other important actors, control of the labor movement is one of the important factors affecting the outcome of the struggle for power in many countries.

Although labor is important and the Soviets are aware of this, their efforts so far have not enabled them to acquire complete control of the trade union movement in most of the non-Communist world. In the highly developed areas which the Soviets claim to see as the most promising, they have had only mixed success at best. In the United States, they have almost no influence in the labor movement. But they have become more sophisticated and are supporting coalitions designed to weaken the antitotalitarian leadership of the AFL-CIO, rather than only attempting to assist Communists to gain influential positions. If they are even partially successful, they will not only weaken the AFL-CIO as a counterweight to their efforts in various parts of the world, but they will also weaken the prodefense establishment in Washington, of which the AFL-CIO is a part.

On the whole, in Northern Europe, West Germany, Britain, and the Benelux countries, they have not been able to secure major influence in the unions, although they have been able to use labor in some of these countries to promote the Soviet concept of detente, to weaken the West economically, and to reduce European interest in defense expenditures. In Southern or Latin Europe, however, they have been the beneficiaries of Communist control of major sections of the labor movement. For the moment, however, the increase of Communist strength has been slowed, and most of the South European Communist Parties are not as responsive to Soviet direction as Moscow would wish. If, however, these Communist Parties should come to dominate the labor movement and the Soviets remain influential, the entire political orientation of the area might very well shift. Labor would not only be available to promote the Soviet concept of detente and other propaganda interests, but it would probably also become an effective part of a major effort to detach Southern Europe from the Western alliance, and enable the Communist Parties to secure a monopoly of political power.

In the less developed areas, where increasingly they see targets of opportunity, the Soviets and their local allies have not, with rare exceptions so far, obtained significant results. Usually, where the labor movement has been almost completely trained and/or financed by the Soviet labor complex, this has come as a result of the local government's close relationship with the Soviet bloc. When this relationship deteriorates, usually the Soviets' close relationship with the local labor movement does, too. But as the years pass, the Soviets are training and financing many thousands of non-Western union officials. While their ability to influence non-Westerners by financing them may not extend very far beyond the last payment, the large number of Soviet bloc-trained union officials may give them important assets in the future. At a minimum, these labor leaders will not be pro-Western and many of them will be pro-Soviet. Many of them can be counted on to assist the Soviets in weakening Western security interests and possibly also to assist local Communist interests.

In some areas, such as parts of Latin America, Africa, and Asia, Western trade unionists, principally American, are training and supporting the local union leaders. But, the Soviets are stepping up their efforts. In other areas, there is no Western trade union presence. In two crucial places, the Persian Gulf and South Africa, for example, the only significant training and support in the labor area comes from the Soviet bloc. As the Persian Gulf industrializes and labor organizations become increasingly important, the Soviets may end up in an increasingly influential position. A postapartheid South Africa would have few Western-oriented black trade union leaders.

Thus, while the Soviets have not been able to gain control of the labor movement in most places, they are continuing to expand their control of this strategically important sector. They already have received some benefits from their efforts; and over the long run, they may be able to acquire an influential base of support in a number of countries. If the West does not continue to provide assistance to non-Communist trade unions which request it, the Soviets will have the entire field to themselves. Western specialists need to know much more about organized labor and the circumstances under which Soviet efforts are and are not effective. They also need to understand why the subject has attracted so little attention in the West, and particularly in the United States. Only then can we decide what precisely to do about the Soviet effort to use labor as one means of shifting the global balance.

Appendix

Major Actors in the International Labor Movement

Global Internationals

WFTU   World Federation of Trade Unions. Soviet-dominated. Created in 1945. Originally the British TUC, the American CIO, and other non-Communist national centers were affiliated, but broke away in 1948–49.

WCL   World Confederation of Labor. Christian-oriented. Originally established in 1920 as International Federation of Christian Trade Unions. Changed its name in 1968.

ICFTU   International Confederation of Free Trade Unions. Now predominantly social democratic. Created in 1949 by the AFL-CIO and non-Communist European national centers which broke with the WFTU. The AFL-CIO withdrew in 1969.

Industrial Internationals

TUIs   Trade Union Internationals. Soviet-dominated. Attached to WFTU.

TIs   Trade Internationals. Attached to WCL.

ITS   International Trade Secretariats. Independent, but on close terms with the ICFTU. About half of the AFL-CIO internationals are affiliated with their respective secretariats.

74

Regional Internationals

ICATU   International Confederation of Arab Trade Unions. Officially nonaligned. Created by the Egyptians in 1956.

AATUF   All-African Trade Union Federation. Officially nonaligned. Created by the "Casablanca group" in 1961, and dissolved in 1976.

OATUU   Organization of African Trade Union Unity. Officially nonaligned. Created in 1973 under the aegis of the Organization of African Unity (OAU).

CPUSTAL   Permanent Committee for Labor Unity in Latin America. Moscow-oriented. Created originally as CUTAL in 1962.

ETUC   European Trade Union Confederation. Created in 1973 by ICFTU affiliates, stressing the common bonds of all European unions.

National Centers

AUCCTU   All-Union Central Council of Trade Unions. Soviet Union, affiliated with WFTU.

CGT   General Confederation of Labor. France, Communist-controlled, affiliated with WFTU.

CGT-FO   "Force Ouvrière." France, non-Communist, affiliated with the ICFTU and the ETUC.

CFTD   French Confederation of Democratic Trade Unions. Formerly Christian, affiliated with WCL and ETUC.

CGIL   Italian Confederation of Labor. Communist-controlled "associate" of the WFTU, and affiliated with the ETUC.

CISL   Italian Confederation of Trade Unions. Christian, affiliated with the ICFTU and ETUC.

UIL   Italian Union of Labor. Socialist and social democratic, affiliated with the ICFTU and ETUC.

TUC   Trades Union Congress. British, primarily Socialist non-Communist, affiliated with the ICFTU and ETUC.

DGB   West German Trade Union Federation. Primarily social democratic, affiliated with the ICFTU and the ETUC.

AFL-CIO   American Federation of Labor-Congress of Industrial Organizations. Withdrew from ICFTU in 1969, but affiliated with the ICFTU's Latin American regional body, ORIT.

National Strategy Information Center, Inc.

STRATEGY PAPERS
Edited by Frank N. Trager and William Henderson
With the assistance of Dorothy E. Nicolosi

The Kremlin and Labor: A Study in National Security Policy by Roy Godson, November 1977

The Evolution of Soviet Security Strategy, 1965-1975 by Avigdor Haselkorn, November 1977

The Geopolitics of the Nuclear Era, by Colin S. Gray, September 1977

The Sino-Soviet Confrontation: Implications for the Future by Harold C. Hinton, September 1976

Food, Foreign Policy, and Raw Materials Cartels by William Schneider, February 1976

Strategic Weapons: An Introduction by Norman Polmar, October 1975

Soviet Sources of Military Doctrine and Strategy by William F. Scott, July 1975

Detente: Promises and Pitfalls by Gerald L. Steibel, March 1975

Oil, Politics, and Sea Power: The Indian Ocean Vortex by Ian W.A.C. Adie, December 1974

The Soviet Presence in Latin America by James D. Theberge, June 1974

The Horn of Africa by J. Bowyer Bell, Jr., December 1973

Research and Development and the Prospects for International Security by Frederick Seitz and Rodney W. Nichols, December 1973

Raw Material Supply in a Multipolar World by Yuan-li Wu, October 1973

The People's Liberation Army: Communist China's Armed Forces by Angus M. Fraser, August 1973 (Out of print)

Nuclear Weapons and the Atlantic Alliance by Wynfred Joshua, May 1973

How to Think About Arms Control and Disarmament by James E. Dougherty, May 1973

The Military Indoctrination of Soviet Youth by Leon Goure, January 1973 (Out of print)

The Asian Alliance: Japan and United States Policy by Franz Michael and Gaston J. Sigur, October 1972

Iran, the Arabian Peninsula, and the Indian Ocean by R. M. Burrell and Alvin J. Cottrell, September 1972 (Out of print)

Soviet Naval Power: Challenge for the 1970s by Norman Polmar, April 1972. Revised edition, September 1974

How Can We Negotiate with the Communists? by Gerald L. Steibel, March 1972 (Out of print)

Soviet Political Warfare Techniques, Espionage and Propaganda in the 1970s by Lyman B. Kirkpatrick, Jr., and Howland H. Sargeant, January 1972

The Soviet Presence in the Eastern Mediterranean by Lawrence L. Whetten, September 1971

The Military Unbalance
Is the U.S. Becoming a Second Class Power? June 1971 (Out of print)

The Future of South Vietnam by Brigadier F. P. Serong, February 1971 (Out of print)

Strategy and National Interests: Reflections for the Future by Bernard Brodie, January 1971 (Out of print)

The Mekong River: A Challenge in Peaceful Development for Southeast Asia by Eugene R. Black, December 1970 (Out of print)

Problems of Strategy in the Pacific and Indian Oceans by George G. Thomson, October 1970

Soviet Penetration into the Middle East by Wynfred Joshua, July 1970. Revised edition, October 1971 (Out of print)

Australian Security Policies and Problems by Justus M. van der Kroef, May 1970 (Out of print)

Detente: Dilemma or Disaster? by Gerald L. Steibel, July 1969 (Out of print)

The Prudent Case for Safeguard by William R. Kintner, June 1969 (Out of print)

AGENDA PAPERS
Edited by Frank N. Trager and William Henderson
With the assistance of Dorothy E. Nicolosi

Understanding the Soviet Military Threat, How CIA Estimates Went Astray by William T. Lee, February 1977

Toward a New Defense for NATO, The Case for Tactical Nuclear Weapons, July 1976

Seven Tracks to Peace in the Middle East by Frank R. Barnett, April 1975

Arms Treaties with Moscow: Unequal Terms Unevenly Applied? by Donald G. Brennan, April 1975

Toward a US Energy Policy by Klaus Knorr, March 1975

Can We Avert Economic Warfare in Raw Materials? US Agriculture as a Blue Chip by William Schneider, July 1974

OTHER PUBLICATIONS

Arms, Men, and Military Budgets, Issues for Fiscal Year 1978 edited by Francis P. Hoeber and William Schneider, Jr., May 1977

Oil, Divestiture and National Security edited by Frank N. Trager, December 1976

Alternatives to Detente by Frank R. Barnett, July 1976

Arms, Men, and Military Budgets, Issues for Fiscal Year 1977 edited by William Schneider, Jr., and Francis P. Hoeber, May 1976

Indian Ocean Naval Limitations, Regional Issues and Global Implications by Alvin J. Cottrell and Walter F. Hahn, April 1976

...NOTES...

...NOTES...

...NOTES...